RAMBLES IN H

CW00549266

Rambles in Hong Kong

by
G.S.P. Heywood

With a New Introduction and Commentary
by Richard Gee

HONG KONG
OXFORD UNIVERSITY PRESS
OXFORD   NEW YORK
1992

Oxford University Press, Hong Kong

Oxford   New York   Toronto
Delhi   Bombay   Calcutta   Madras   Karachi
Kuala Lumpur   Singapore   Hong Kong   Tokyo
Nairobi   Dar es Salaam   Cape Town
Melbourne   Auckland   Madrid

and associated companies in
Berlin   Ibadan

Oxford is a trade mark of Oxford University Press

First published 1992

Published in the United States
by Oxford University Press, New York

© Oxford University Press 1992

All rights reserved. No part of this publication may be reproduced,
stored in a retrieval system, or transmitted, in any form or by any means,
without the prior permission in writing of Oxford University Press.
Within Hong Kong, exceptions are allowed in respect of any fair dealing for the
purpose of research or private study, or criticism or review, as permitted
under the Copyright Ordinance, 1956. Enquiries concerning
reproduction outside these terms and in other countries should be
sent to Oxford University Press at the address below

This book is sold subject to the condition that it shall not, by way
of trade or otherwise, be lent, re-sold, hired out or otherwise circulated
without the publisher's prior consent in any form of binding or cover
other than that in which it is published and without a similar condition
including this condition being imposed on the subsequent purchaser

British Library Cataloguing in Publication Data
available

Library of Congress Cataloging in Publication Data
Heywood, G.S.P.
Rambles in Hong Kong / by G.S.P. Heywood ; with a new introduction
and commentary by Richard Gee.
p. cm. – (Oxford in Asia paperbacks)
ISBN 0–19–585816–6
1. Hiking–Hong Kong –Guidebooks.
2. Hong Kong–Guidebooks.
I. Gee, Richard. II. Title. III. Series.
GV199.44.H85H49   1992
915. 125–dc20

Printed in Hong Kong
Published by Oxford University Press
18/F Warwick House, Tong Chong Street, Quarry Bay, Hong Kong

PREFACE

I CAME across Graham Heywood's book shortly after I arrived in Hong Kong in 1986. It immediately became my walking companion, and I grew to cherish its charming stories of a vanished world. Graham loved the hills and the countryside, and his love struck a responsive chord in me.

Since no decent book about the hills was in print, I decided I ought to write one. It seems to be a Hong Kong habit. Graham had the same idea when he arrived sixty years ago in 1932; and thousands of others have been inspired to try singing the glories of this place in one way or another. Eventually I hit on the idea of reprinting the original *Rambles in Hong Kong* with a new parallel text, updating and adding to the old one.

It's now fifty-four years since the first edition of *Rambles* was published in December 1938. It would have been an ideal Christmas present, selling for just $2. The book was a revised and expanded version of a series of articles Graham wrote for the *Hong Kong Naturalist* magazine between May 1935 and December 1936.

Most copies of both the book and the magazine were lost during the war years, and so after the war, he updated and reissued the book to take account of some of the changes around him. The second edition, published in 1951, was written with the first edition in front of him for inspiration. As a result, he left many sections and sentences unchanged from the first edition, while rewriting others. All eleven black-and-white photographs from the first edition were omitted, probably to keep costs down. Also discarded was his original first paragraph:

This is a book for walkers; it attempts to cater for all tastes, for the
expeditions described range from real mountain climbs, such as the ·
ascent of the north face of Ma On Shan, to gentle afternoon walks,
such as a stroll in the Lam Tsun Valley or the Ping Shan marshes. Perhaps
there is no need for a book of this kind; those who love the country can
explore it without being told the way. But I have found so much
happiness and such enrichment of life in leisure hours spent in the
country, that in gratitude I must tell of its joys, and perhaps in so doing
may persuade others to go out and find these delights for themselves.

Many times in the last year I have put aside my own efforts, feeling inadequate and despairing of ever being able to match up to Graham. His writing is so refreshingly free from blather. I can almost hear him talking to me as I struggle up through the jungle in search of his `obvious track'.

Each time, I've had to start again because I end up with exactly the same feeling. It's been a joy to discover his Hong Kong. Even though so much has gone, there's still a lot left for us to enjoy in these 400 square miles.

Guidebooks to mountains take two forms. First, there's the detailed approach, where the author tells you exactly where to go—'left here, right there', and so on. Then there's the second sort, which just waves vaguely in the direction of the hills and leaves the rest up to the walker.

When I first arrived in Hong Kong, I thought I would write the first sort of book, like Alfred Wainwright did so masterfully for the English Lake District in *Pictorial Guides to the Lakeland Fells*—seven volumes with detailed descriptions of every route, every ridge walk, and every view for every single summit. At some point, I realised that my idea was hopelessly unrealistic, and that such a book would never get to press.

Some sensible books in this category are available now, and they're good when you want a straightforward walk or when you've got a strict deadline. Earlier efforts in this line have been superseded by Kaarlo Schepel's three-volume *Magic Walks* series, which has detailed directions for a variety of easy walks. The problem with the detailed approach to guidebooks is that they rapidly become out of date as the countryside changes.

Rambles is the second sort of guidebook. You won't get precise step-by-step instructions unless there's a very good safety reason for it. Graham, who was an accomplished and adventurous climber, described some of his walks in little more than a few brief words. Even though finding routes away from the beaten track was tricky then, and is much more so today, I think he got the balance right, so I'm sticking to it. I'm going to be as vague in places as an old Scottish guidebook which says 'start on this side of the hill and finish on the other side.'

Sometimes I think we're softer than our ancestors; so many of the interesting old paths that they used to follow have been abandoned, while easier and more convenient routes are now overused. There are three factors. First, we have less time—or we think we do; actually we have the same amount, but we choose to spend it in different ways. Second, we travel more, and more people travel, and we all want to see the same places, so most visitors end up starting from the same spot. Finally, we are now able to rely on accurate maps, whereas in Graham's day you had to make your own way to a much greater extent.

How should you use this book, then? It has three elements to it.

First, the left-hand page is Graham's 1951 text. I hope you will share my enjoyment in reading his stories of the pre-war Hong Kong countryside. If it inspires you to get out onto the hills and try his expeditions, take the book with you and read his stories as you walk. Some of them don't need any updating. His description of the ridge walk from Kowloon Peak to Ma On Shan, for example, is still a perfectly adequate guide. On the other hand, some of his walks are mere echoes of days long gone. His recommended approach route to Lion Rock from the south always leaves me struggling to imagine what it must have been like.

Second, the right-hand page is my own text, which supplements Graham's. If I have not commented on a particular walk, you may assume that I have tried it and found it feasible. My main aim has been to warn you of changes and help you to explore successfully. I do not want to deter you from trying any of Graham's walks; quite the reverse.

Some of my text points you in the direction of hills and places that Graham didn't mention, such as Kai Keung Leng in the northwest, or parts of Sai Kung Country Park. And some of my own experiences on the hills have barged their way in; a mix of good and bad, they are here in the hope that you may be forewarned, inspired, or entertained.

The final element is an examination of the changes to the Hong Kong countryside over the last sixty years. My Chapter II includes an overview of these changes. A series of inserts looks at some specific items, and includes a selection of old newspaper articles, quotes, and snippets. Most refer to hills in one way or another. One or two just tickled my fancy.

The major change for ramblers is in the extent of the vegetation on the hills. As you explore, you will realise that many of Graham's walks would not have been possible in the casual way he describes if there had been the same amount of vegetation that now chokes the slopes and blocks progress almost everywhere except along established paths. There are very few places now where you can step so insouciantly as Graham, confident that you'll find a route somehow. Woe to the rambler who recklessly seeks short-cuts.

The valleys, the villages, and the cities have changed tremendously. There are not many places where Hong Kong's past survives. Hong Kong lives a full life, looking forward, not back. That is clearly a blessing, because it has brought prosperity and a chance of a better life to so many. It is also a curse, because the urge to progress has steadily been destroying the environment and making it harder to find peace and quiet.

But Graham's philosophy, which I share, was that peace cannot be destroyed. It is within us, and it's there when we want to find it, whatever the external circumstances. Rambling the hills is just one way of getting a little more mellow, so that we are open to recognise the treasure within.

PREFACE

When I first read *Rambles* five years ago, I was struck by the way in which the author's personality was projected so strongly. What a nice chap he must have been, I kept thinking. At that time, I had no idea who Graham Heywood was; the book doesn't give any hints. So I started researching, and the more I found, the more my initial impression was confirmed. It has been a most rewarding adventure. Every reference I've found has been favourable. Every personal recollection has been warm. Graham was liked and admired by everyone I've spoken to. In Chapter II, therefore, besides the survey of Hong Kong 1932–92, I've taken a quick look at Graham Heywood, 1903–85.

Many people have contributed to this book. I am especially grateful to Graham's two daughters, Susan and Veronica. With enthusiasm, patience, and frankness, they have fed me with stories, answered my questions, given me shelter, confirmed everything I discovered about their father, and encouraged me to produce this book.

Long-time Hong Kong residents have played important roles. Pat Loseby, who was a little girl in Stanley Camp, told me stories of her youth and put me in touch with Susan Heywood. Ronnie Ross ('never much of a walker', in his own words) recounted graphic memories of post-war Hong Kong. Bill Smyly, who was always a walker, shared his Christmas pudding and told me all about what the hills were like when he arrived in the 1950s. The Royal Observatory let me search through their records and talk to the only member of the staff who was there at the same time as Graham; and it was in their basement that I first discovered what the 'G.S.P.' stands for—Graham Scudamore Percival. Elizabeth Sinn of Hong Kong University found time to talk to me despite her busy schedule, giving me encouragement and a copy of R.C. Hurley's delightful 1896 walking guide.

When I had done most of the walks and my notes for the book were well advanced, a lovely coincidence led me to Oxford University Press. Susan Heywood was passing through Hong Kong with her husband in early 1991. I took her to an exhibition of old photographs and introduced her to Valerie Garrett, a fellow-enthusiast of old Hong Kong. I explained to Valerie that I wanted to reissue *Rambles*. 'But I'm reissuing it!' she exclaimed. Unknown to me, and unaware herself of my intentions, she had been trying to persuade OUP to reissue it. OUP liked the book but was reluctant to publish it without some updating. Valerie is not a walker, so I took over her negotiations with OUP, and here we are.

Others have inspired me to walk and to write. When I was a toddler, my parents showed me that climbing hills was just a matter of one foot in front of the other until you can't go any higher. Sister Joyce of Matilda Hospital and Lisa Chan of 'Huppy

Handbook' let me in on the secret that writing a book is just a question of starting and then continuing until you finish.

My girlfriend Singeng has been terrific. She's a city girl, a once-in-a-while walker, and sometimes my obsession with this project has had her baffled. She's been deserted at the weekend while I rambled, and neglected at night while I wrote. She was worried sick one weekend when I disappeared on an unscheduled overnight bivouac. In return, she's welcomed me home, inspired me to write, edited my first attempts, cajoled me, scolded me, and even, sometimes, walked with me. Our outings together have all been memorable—some of them are in the book. Thank you, Singeng.

This is not meant to be a definitive guide or an instruction manual, and I would feel nervous if anybody tried to use it like that. I'll be content if you put this book by your favourite easy chair, and read it for inspiration. Daydream. Imagine 'what if . . .' Study the old map on a winter evening. Plot a totally new route for yourself. Go and check it out. It might be OK; it might not. If it is, congratulate yourself. If it isn't, retrace your steps and try again.

The love of mountains is an eternal theme of Chinese poetry. Li Bai, the famous Tang dynasty poet, wrote that: 'All my life I have loved to roam on the famous mountains.'

A Song dynasty poet, Feng Shixing, wrote of Mount Omei, one of China's holy mountains:

> Cliffs and mountain peaks—all seen for the first time;
> The grasses and trees!—half of them are nameless.
> Green the sharp slopes, hill upon hill of jade;
> In the wavering light, tree after tree of emerald.
> Clouds among the ranges keep pace with the visitor's sleeve;
> Echoes through the valley answer the monk's chanting.
> In the perfect stillness I am bemused and sleepless;
> Over the empty mountain the moon is brightly gleaming.

'First Night on Mount Omei', translated by
D. L. Phelps and M. K. Wilmott in *Pilgrimage in Poetry to Mount Omei*.

Su Dong-po, one of China's most famous poets, also wrote on Mount Omei in the Song dynasty:

> O but having bodily leisure—that is to be an Immortal!
> Before my eyes black streams and white break their bounds and scatter.
> Please, sir, try sitting among the rocky peaks—
> One day will be the same as 500 years.

'Temple of the White Waters', also from
Pilgrimage in Poetry to Mount Omei.

CONTENTS

PLATES AND ILLUSTRATIONS

MAPS

INTRODUCTION.

This little book first appeared some twelve years ago; it was intended for walkers and country-lovers, and there still seems to be a demand for it. In the present edition the text has been revised, and descriptions of a few new expeditions have been added; most of the pages, however, appear as they were originally written when the recollection of carefree days on the hills was fresh in my mind.

In the last two or three years a good many changes have taken place in the New Territories which are not mentioned here; new roads have been built, and certain military areas are now closed to the public. But most of the country is still accessible to walkers, and though there have been unsightly developments here and there much of it remains wild and unspoilt.

The descriptions of walks are in nearly every case from personal knowledge, and the times given are exclusive of halts and refer to an average walker; a fast goer can probably reduce them by one-third. Country things are mentioned in passing—the birds and the flowers, village life, farming, fishing and local crafts. The following books may be consulted for fuller and more expert information about the country. In the "Hong Kong Naturalist", a quarterly journal published before the war and now unfortunately out of print, will be found a store of knowledge about birds, beasts and fishes, flowers and trees, archaeology and folk-lore. Its editor, Dr. G. A. C. Herklots, has recently re-issued a great deal of this information in "The Hong Kong Countryside"—a delightfully written book which will appeal to any country-lover. "Hong Kong in its Geographical Setting", by Dr. S. G. Davis, deals with the geology, geography and climate of the Colony.

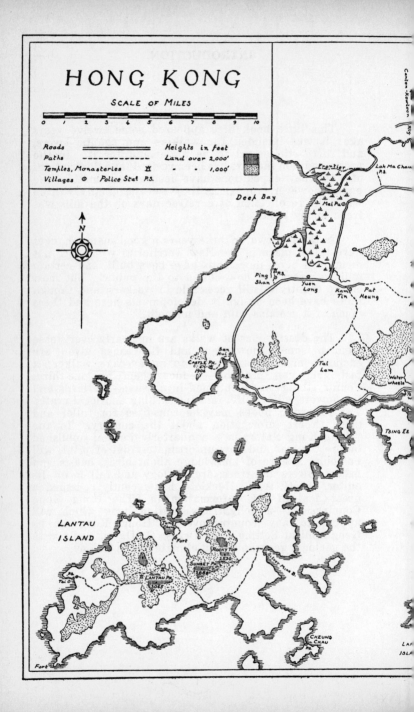

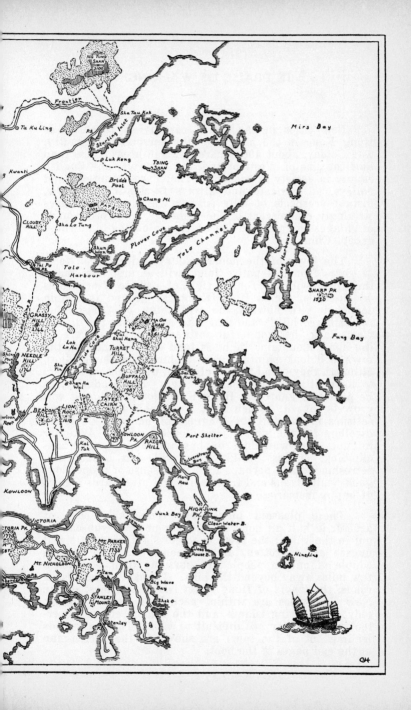

CHAPTER I.

IN PRAISE OF WALKING.

Few cities in the world can be so favoured as Hong Kong in the beauty of the surrounding country. The Colony, about 400 square miles in area, is less than half the size of Westmorland, but can rival any English county in variety of scenery. There are mountains and valleys, an intricate and always fascinating coastline, distant prospects of hilly islands which are sometimes strikingly reminiscent of the Hebrides, and foregrounds of villages and paddy fields which can belong to nowhere except China.

The lover of the home country, exiled for a term of years from his native land, will at first miss many things; he will long for the sight of a glade of primroses or bluebells, for in Hong Kong the ground is seldom carpeted with flowers; he will think of "those blue remembered hills", and find with regret that the distant views lack the wonderful softness and atmosphere of the home mountains; if he is fond of old buildings, the town will look painfully raw to him, and the villages, although they blend admirably with the landscape, seem to have little of the charm of age. But gradually, as he comes to know the Hong Kong countryside, he will grow to love it. Much of it is serenely beautiful, and satisfies to the full the longings of many of us town-dwellers for the simple joys of the country. Whether he goes bird-watching, or bug-hunting, or mountain-climbing, or just walking, he will find beauty and refreshment, and perhaps a renewed sense of proportion; good health is his and friendship, and afterwards a store of happy memories.

These pleasant places are remarkably easy of access; in half an hour by bus, car or train you can be out in the wilds; the town is out of sight, its bustle and unease are forgotten, and it seems incredible that a couple of million people are pursuing their business a few miles away beyond the hills. Thanks to the various roads, the whole of Hong Kong Island and most of the New Territories are within reach in a day's walking; only the outlying islands and the remote country over-looking Mirs Bay are difficult to visit. The main-roads leading out of the town are shown in the sketch-map at the end pages of the book.

Commentary—Chapter 1

MUCH has changed in the last sixty years, but Hong Kong's hills still provide joy to those who walk there. Midnight and dawn are still magical. The views are still magnificent. And the soul can still derive the utmost refreshment from these wonderful surroundings.

Pause for a little while and reconsider the potential of your surroundings: the joy of sunrise on a hilltop; strolling through a quiet valley with a loved one, just the birds in the trees for company; simple pleasures that refresh the soul. Here in Hong Kong, away from the streets and the shops and the people, we can still find close at hand the beauty and refreshment, and the renewed sense of proportion, that Graham so eloquently praises.

Access to the hills is even easier now. Roads and public transport make it possible to get to virtually anywhere in the territory within a few hours of leaving the city centre. The government publishes an annual compendium of bus and ferry timetables, which is invaluable at the planning stage. The New Territories is well served by minibuses connecting urban centres and remote villages.

This book is chiefly for explorers. As you use it, you will become an explorer, even if you are not already. Be prepared to get lost several times in the course of a day and to add time for relocation. To find wilder places, we venture off beaten tracks; the adventurous spirit is rewarded with surprises round every corner—not always pleasantly, mind.

What to take is simple. Food and drink—whatever you want. Water is essential. Although there are shops with drinks in the villages and at a few places like Sha Tin Pass above Kowloon, there are no shops on the hills. In summer, in particular, dehydration is a very real danger if you walk for just a few hours without drinking. When you're not sure where your route will take you, it's wise to have plenty of water with you—and make sure you drink it. If you're wandering away from major trails, take a little extra food as emergency rations.

Shorts are fine for the Maclehose Trail and other well-trodden paths, but long trousers are best for exploring. Long-sleeved shirts protect arms and can be rolled up when it's hot.

Footwear for walkers is a much-debated topic, and views tend to be strongly held. Technology has done wonders for our feet, and very few people wear nailed boots these days; even rock climbers can get terrific grip with special rubber soles. Some walkers wear boots. Some wear running shoes. Trainers are common. When it's dry underfoot, almost anything will do. When it's muddy, walking is much easier if the sole has some kind of tread.

Maps have improved since 1938. The best modern maps are the Countryside Series; seven sheets covering the whole territory, all at 1:25,000 except for the smaller islands (various scales). Designed for walkers and others using the countryside, they show great detail, and are regularly updated. Sheet No. 5 (North-East New Territories) won an international prize a few

A word of warning; robberies and crimes of violence were frequent immediately after the war, and though the police have done magnificent work in restoring law and order, are not entirely unknown at the time of writing. If you are walking in the country, it is just as well to go in a party of not less than four, to leave any valuables behind, and to avoid the immediate neighbourhood of the town. But the ordinary countryman is a friendly creature, who usually has a smiling welcome for any foreigner walking through his village.

What to take. For a whole day's expedition you will want food and drink. The latter is always a problem; bottles are heavy, and thermoses have a horrid habit of breaking and inundating the contents of your rucksack with coffee. Perhaps the best plan is to carry a store of the local oranges; they are delicious, and are in season through most of the winter. To drink deep of a clear mountain stream after a long hot climb is one of life's greatest blisses; be sure, however, that your drinking place is above the upper limit of cultivation.

Rocks and thickets are hard on clothes, and it is well to wear old ones. Though it is seldom too cold to walk in shorts, a spare coat or woolly will often be found very acceptable while halting on a summit.

As to footwear, rubber-soled shoes are admirable in dry weather, but are apt to slip on wet or greasy rocks. I prefer nailed shoes; provided the nails are not too worn, they will grip on any surface wet or dry. Unfortunately they make a terrible clatter on cobbled paths, which is a disadvantage when you are birdwatching or attempting to sneak past a village without arousing the dogs.

A map is the walker's best friend; it accompanies him on his rambles, guides him when in doubt, and gives him many happy hours at home re-living past days on the hills or planning new ones. Several maps of the Colony have been published by the War Office, but are not always obtainable at the booksellers. The handiest is the 1936 map of Hong Kong and the New Territories, in one sheet on a scale of 1:80,000 (about ¼ inch to a mile). A far more detailed map is the beautiful R.A.F. survey of 1931, published in 24 sheets on a scale of 1:20,000.

The Names of the Hills

I've always been fascinated by the names of the hills. Graham wrote that English names are prosaic, and voted for adopting native names wherever possible. Nearly all of Hong Kong's hills have at least one Chinese name, often more, as well as their Western name. As far as I can, I have included Chinese names and translations. This is not always easy, of course; imagine doing it in reverse. Graham cites Scafell Pike and Everest, but how would you translate those into Chinese? What do they mean? Names often don't seem to mean anything, so don't take my rough and ready guesses as authoritative translations.

One authority on names is the Hong Kong Gazetteer, *published in 1958, with this fairly scathing introduction by K. M. A. Barnett:*

Anybody whose work takes him into the rural parts of Hong Kong will soon be made aware of the badness of the maps. The errors in cartographical detail I must leave to the cartographer to explain. The errors which concern me are those in the nomenclature. It is apparent after the most cursory check that a large proportion of the place-names are incorrect—either the wrong name, or the right name wrongly spelt, or the right name in the wrong place.

Barnett went on to speculate about the origins of the Chinese characters used in place names, concluding that extensive borrowing from dialects and earlier hill tribes, and the propensity of spoken language to distort meaning, meant that a large number of common words in place names were not the originals. I take comfort from the fact that even an expert was confused and doubtful about them.

Why were there so many mistakes? Some were due to a lack of competent linguists, says Barnett:

Field survey parties have had to rely on less than the best interpreters, or even on pidgin English, with some amusing results in the early days. It was for this reason that the island of Ma Shi Chau is still marked on some maps as No Kot Choi—i.e. No got choy, pidgin English for 'No food to be had'.

Later surveyors, says Barnett, knew some Chinese, but found it hard to cope with dialects—Tanka, Hoklo, two versions of Cantonese, three kinds of Hakka—when it came to place names:

To this difficulty, combined with a simple misprint, is to be attributed the map name of the mountain north of the Lam Tsuen Valley. It is Tai To Yan—Razor Cliff. The Nam Tau dialect pronounces this Tai Tau Yang, which became Tai Tan Yang by misreading the final letter of Tau. . . . Even with field workers who are fluent in the local languages, it is not easy to keep the record straight. Country people the world over take a delight in mystifying strangers. Add to this the Chinese convention against direct question and answer, and it will be seen that the

Continued on page 9

A compass may be useful if you are caught in a mist on high ground, as often happens in spring. There is little danger of becoming completely lost, however, as there are no wide moorlands, and if you lose your way on a clouded mountain-top it is merely necessary to walk downhill to reach the valley.

Some people advise carrying potassium permanganate to apply to snake-bites. Although there are venomous snakes in the Colony, few of them are aggressive, and the risk of being bitten is extremely small, particularly in the winter.

A rucksack is almost essential for carrying odds and ends; pockets are too small, and a haversack is continually catching on bushes and rocks.

Seasons and Weather. Without doubt the autumn is the best season for walking in Hong Kong. Some enthusiasts make a point of going their first long walk on the Double Tenth holiday at the beginning of October, though often it is still too hot for anything very energetic. November and December are ideal—fine, cool and bracing. There is plenty of sunshine, and the landscapes are full of vivid colour. The air has come from far away north, and still carries with it a hint of the snowy uplands of Manchuria and Siberia over which it has blown.

After the New Year low cloud becomes prevalent; the hill-tops are often shrouded in clammy mists, as dwellers on the Peak know only too well. Unless you enjoy finding your way over clouded mountain tops by map and compass, it is better to confine your walks to lower ground, exploring the valleys and passes. The skies are grey, and the colour-scheme of the countryside is more subdued than in the bright autumn days, but there is a feeling of spring in the air, and tender greens are beginning to show in the woods side by side with the reds and browns of autumn. For here there is no dead season when the trees are bare and the wild creatures are asleep or hushed and numbed with the cold; even in February, the coldest month of the year, there are flowers to be found, and some of the birds are starting to nest.

chances of a surveyor, working against time, getting a correct list of the names of topographical features, or even of the chief villages, are not good. The wonder is not that there are so many mistakes, but that any of the names are right. Finally, the best maps (such as they are) are not readily available even to many public servants, and the mountaineer and hiker, from whom corrections might come, often has to content himself with an old battered copy of an extinct edition.

Where do names come from? The original Chinese names came from fung shui men and farmers. A few hills, the more prominent ones, might have been named by travellers. For the fung shui man, a good name is as important as a good location, and the wrong name can bring trouble even on a good spot. The second names came from the army's strategic planners, for whom identification was essential. An officer ordering his troops to occupy 'that hill over there' doesn't get results. The soldiers who have to dig in quickly christen their new homes with private names like Dog Hill or Princess Hill, for example.

Local names are rare in two areas. The first area is the north side of Hong Kong island, perhaps because there were few farmers on that side before 1840, and the Chinese who came after 1840 were interested in business, not hills; the island's hills now have local spellings of the colonists' Western names. The second area is the northern New Territories, where the army sprinkled names all over the countryside; farmers only named the hills near their villages.

Not all the names appear on maps, because mapmakers can't fit them all. As farming and fighting communities disappear, therefore, names and histories are probably disappearing. Farmers name their land, but don't record the names anywhere. The histories of some of the farming families go back for centuries, to the time nearly a thousand years ago when they first arrived, but they record the names of important people, not hills. Soldiers retire, new troops invent new names, and old ones are forgotten. Hills enter the military record only if they become battlegrounds.

The 1958 Gazetteer was not the first. Imperial officials posted away from home to all parts of China needed help in their new posts. Written gazetteers became an invaluable guide for newcomers who didn't speak the local dialects. The New Peace County Gazetteer of 1819 covered the Hong Kong area; New Peace County, by Peter Y. L. Ng, (Hong Kong University Press, 1983) translates some of the more interesting entries.

In April the weather is becoming unpleasantly damp and hot, and in May summer is with us in earnest. From then until the end of September it is really too hot for any strenuous scrambling, and only those with stout hearts and thick skulls can attempt mountain ascents under the fiery summer sun. But many delights remain to the country lover—strolling through villages, watching the farmers at their sowing and harvesting, or exploring some hill stream, with a halt for a bathe in a clear pool under a waterfall. And then there is always the sea; all those miles of rocky coast and sandy beaches. Near the main-roads the latter are populous in hot weather, and are often disfigured by dreadful little concrete bathing huts, but away from the beaten track plenty of beaches remain unfrequented.

The summer is the rainy season; the weather is often showery, and sometimes the downpours are of tropical intensity. But when the sun shines, as it very frequently does, our countryside is undoubtedly more beautiful in summer than at other seasons of the year. Gone are the clear bright hardness of the views in autumn and the grey skies of spring; the land no longer looks parched and dried up, as it does in winter. Instead there is a wealth of colour in the landscape; the woods and shrubs are clothed in luxuriant foliage, the sea is an unforgettable blue, and the fields, which in winter were the dull brown of dead stubble, have now come to life with the vivid green of the young rice—a marvellous colour, greener even than an English lawn. And the skies are magnificent; great cumulus clouds rest on the mountain tops, and tower up in billows of dazzling white into the deep blue of the heaven.

As Viscount Grey once said, "It is always some sort of a day in the country", and so the seasons pass pleasantly enough. Autumn comes again, and we unearth our woolly clothes and our hobnailed shoes and set out for the hills once more.

years ago. They're published by the Survey & Mapping Office of the Buildings & Lands Department, which also does a series of 16 sheets at the slightly larger scale of 1:20,000. These maps are inaccurate, misleading, and out of date. People do use them, but I don't know why. Various other maps are available, but none is suitable for explorers. Forget them. Buildings & Lands also produces a 1:100,000 map which has the whole territory on one sheet, giving a clear picture of how it all fits together.

You can buy Countryside Series maps at the Government Publications Bookshop in the Central General Post Office, and at the South China Morning Post Bookshop at the Star Ferry. They only cost about $20. You can also get them direct from Buildings & Lands, on the 14th floor of the Murray Building. When you go there, give yourself an hour or so and ask to see their historical maps. They have a big collection of maps dating back to the 1840s, from which they will make Xerox copies for about $20 each. They've got the maps that Graham refers to, the 1931 RAF survey; it's fascinating to trace his walks on the same maps that he used.

For hills over the border, you need different maps. Universal Publications publishes a *Map of Pearl Delta*, which shows very general contours and covers a large area at a scale of 1:400,000, and *Map of Shenzhen*, which uses shading to indicate hills, has more names (in Chinese), and covers only Shenzhen at an unspecified scale, about 1:130,000. The old 1931 RAF survey extends 15 kilometres north of the border; it's intriguing to look at, but it isn't any practical use.

I have given the six-digit grid reference in brackets for some of the walks. All the Buildings & Lands maps use a standard grid.

Let's consider safety on the hills. There are three important points to remember:

• If you're walking alone, leave a note of your route with someone reliable and agree on an emergency procedure in case you do get into trouble.
• Take emergency equipment, including a torch and a first aid kit, and know how to use it.
• If conditions get bad, reassess the situation. Turn back before it's too late. You can always try again another day.

Should you walk alone or with others? If you're new at the game, company is comforting, especially when you're exploring and don't know what you'll find. As you get more experienced, I think it's a matter of personal preference.

CHAPTER II.

THE LIE OF THE LAND.

C. E. Montague describes how you can piece together in your mind a complete picture of the whole length and breadth of England by ascending to a few notable viewpoints, and seeing for yourself the lie of the land. You realize how small England is, and how rich in scenery, and through the knowledge thus gained you can attain a deeper love for the country.

It is the same with any good corner of the world —to know it completely is to grow fond of it; familiarity breeds not disdain but affection. In Hong Kong it is an easy matter; almost the whole Colony can be seen from one commanding height, and in this chapter I will try to give you an idea of the lie of the land. So let us imagine ourselves to be on the top of Tai Mo Shan, a mountain which is admirably suited for our purpose, for it is the highest in the Colony and is the central hub from which radiate the lesser ridges on the mainland. The sketch map in the end pages of this book will help you to follow the description.

South-eastward from the summit the ground falls away to Pineapple Pass, overlooking Shing Mun Reservoir. The watershed continues southward to the low saddle by Kowloon Reservoir, and then rises to the long curving ridge of the Kowloon Hills—the "Nine Dragons", whose familiar skyline shuts away the town from the country to the north. Separated from us by Tide Cove is a branch of this ridge, which leaves the Kowloon range at Tate's Cairn and runs northward over Buffalo Hill to Ma On Shan, the most beautiful of our mountains.

Beyond this line of hills, and mostly out of sight from our viewpoint, is a stretch of wild remote country running out towards Mirs Bay in two long peninsulas, between the sea inlets of Junk Bay, Port Shelter and Tolo Channel. Unspoilt, and until recently almost inaccessible, this country is to my mind by far the most lovely part of the Colony. And yet, as I write this, a picture of the Lam Tsun valley comes into my mind, very fair to look on; I am not sure that it does not come first in my affections. Who can choose between the Elysian fields?

Commentary—Chapter 2

HONG KONG and its surrounding countryside looked very different in 1932, when Graham arrived in Hong Kong to join the Royal Observatory, after the Depression had forced the cancellation of an Antarctic expedition on which he had been accepted as meteorologist. Hong Kong was in the middle of a drought. The population was about 900,000, most of whom lived in rural areas and villages in the New Territories, still relatively backward and undeveloped. Only 10 per cent of rural people could read or write. Only 5,000 country children went to school.

In *At The Peak* (MacMillan, 1983), Paul Gillingham's vivid portrayal of daily life between the wars, Hong Kong emerges as a sleepy coastal port with some land attached, not very important to the rest of the world. Hong Kong's original role as the West's entrepot to China had been lost when Shanghai began to prosper.

Since then, of course, Hong Kong has been transformed into a bustling international giant. The most dramatic changes came in the first post-war decade, when the Communists won the civil war on the mainland, and Shanghai was abandoned by its international community and its Chinese industrialists. Shanghai's loss was Hong Kong's gain, and after a brief hiccup when China trade almost disappeared during the Korean War, Hong Kong never looked back.

Graham became Director of the Royal Observatory in 1946 and stayed until 1955. During the first half of that period, Hong Kong's population grew from 600,000 to two and a half million. Most of the new arrivals were penniless and starving, and both Graham and his wife Valerie got involved. Veronica recounts how 'my mother set up the welfare centre for the homeless refugees, providing milk powder, food, birth control advice, equipment for work, and care for the abandoned, & once a year a BUMPER party when she enrolled the army & navy to help . . . & Daddy.'

Just as Hong Kong grew and matured, so did the Observatory under Graham's directorship. By the time he retired, he had established it as one of the leading and most reliable sources of weather information in Asia. On the strength of his books and scientific papers, Graham became one of the world's experts on typhoons.

During Graham's time, the hills and valleys were much more barren than they are now, and it was much easier for Graham to follow the paths. The valleys were filled with rice paddy, wet, green, and muddy in the summer, dry, bleak and hard in the winter. There was no vegetation between the fields, and very little elsewhere. Old photographs of the New Territories in winter depict desolate plains, the only vegetation being *fung shui* groves behind the villages.

Graham describes how the villagers burnt the grass on the hilltops every year for ashes to fertilise their fields. The village women regularly harvested the grass on the slopes as fuel for cooking. Graham likens the women with their loads of grass to 'miniature haystacks'.

North-eastward from our viewpoint is the narrow gap between the foot of Tai Mo Shan and the beginning of the Pat Sin range; the latter stretches away for miles in a bold escarpment overlooking the northern shore of Tolo Harbour. Behind it is the Sha Tau Kok valley and Starling Inlet (you are never far from an inlet of the sea in Hong Kong), and beyond them again is the big mountain Ng Tung Shan, just within Chinese territory, with its attendant foothills.

Close beneath Tai Mo Shan to the north and the north-west are the two wide and fertile valleys of Lam Tsun and Pat Heung, bounded on the far side by the lower hills overlooking Fanling. The Pat Heung valley drains into the marshes bordering Deep Bay. This is very different country from the rest of the New Territories; the high hills are left behind, giving place to a long coastal belt of low-lying ground, extending from the Shum Chun estuary almost to Castle Peak. Here are the richest paddy fields, and the salt marshes inhabited only by lonely fishing people and rare birds. A district with a peculiar charm, though it lacks the wild beauty of the hills.

Turning to the west, we look out over a confused range of bare and rocky hills towards Castle Peak, which stands at the westernmost point of the mainland.

There remain the islands, of which there are a hundred or so, large and small, within British waters. There is always something romantic about islands, and these islands of ours add immeasurably to the beauty of the seaward views.

The scenery of a district and even its domestic architecture usually depend to a large extent on the nature of the underlying rock, as for example in the chalk and limestone belts of England. In Hong Kong we are lucky to have such variety of landscape, for the underlying rock is almost exclusively granite. Near the surface this rock decomposes into a reddish subsoil, of the consistency of hard cheese, which can be seen in any cutting along the roads. The decomposed granite produces the familiar red soil of the hillsides, which is the bane of gardeners, for it cakes hard in the sun and is almost impervious to water. Given time, however, for the formation of humus, this soil can carry a very rich vegatation.

In the years just before the war, unauthorised tree-cutting became a problem. Then the last few trees on the hills were chopped down during the war for construction and fuel.

Three major post-war population movements transformed the countryside. In the first, remote villages in the New Territories and on outlying islands were abandoned as the younger generation moved to the city or went abroad. Some villages survived; their 'remittance houses' were built in the 1960s with money sent back by those running restaurants, laundries, and trading businesses abroad.

In the second movement, refugee farmers from China took over the more accessible agricultural areas, and became tenants of the old clan landlords. They still farm, but rice has been replaced by vegetables and by more intensive market gardening. In marginal areas, squatters have moved in and extended cultivation up the hillsides.

In the third major population movement, the city has moved to the country. New towns have been built—at Tsuen Wan, Tuen Mun, Yuen Long, Tin Shui Wai, Fanling, Sheung Shui, Tai Po, Sha Tin, and Junk Bay. Some of the development has involved uprooting or submerging traditional rural communities, but a vast number of people now live on land that simply wasn't there before. Reclamation has given Hong Kong a new shape, and in the process given the old countryside new transport, new industries, new shopping centres, new ways of life.

As people left the villages and abandoned rice farming, the hillsides began to turn green. Grass grew tall, and shrubs took hold. The government built roads, even to remote areas, so that minibuses and trucks could get access. People stopped walking from one village to another, so the old trails became disused and overgrown. Then the government started planting trees, completely masking some of the paths as they worked to stabilise eroded slopes.

The ancestral graves on the hillsides got less attention from relatives. The newcomers from China, of course, had no interest in other families' graves, and ignored them. The old people who stayed on in the villages weren't able to look after them as much as before. Visits from the youngsters were restricted to Ching Ming in the spring, and Chung Yeung in the autumn. Then people living overseas started to take away their ancestor's bones for relocation near their new homes—they could take better care of them, and it was good *fung shui* for their future. So even the little paths leading out of the villages up the hillsides to the graves gradually got forgotten, and the *fung shui* groves spread and choked the lower slopes.

The valleys and coastal areas have been the site for a further development. As land in the urban area has grown steadily more expensive, it has become worthwhile for business to expand out of town. Containers, for example, can be stored in a field just as well as in a port. Old cars can be driven a few extra miles to the country before they are dumped and scavenged for spare

It is the granite which gives the characteristic outlines to our hills, with their hummocky tops and their sides carved by erosion into numerous ribs and gullies. The Hong Kong mountains are not very high, but some of them are extraordinarily good to look on; few mountain views can compare with the Pat Sin range seen across Tolo Harbour on a summer evening, when the level sunlight throws the modelling of the hillsides into delicate relief and the summit ridge stands up bold and clear against the blue sky.

The harder portions of the granite have withstood decomposition, and appear on the surface as rocky outcrops and detached boulders scattered over the hills. Some of these outcrops of harder rock form magnificent crags, as for instance on Lion Rock, Kowloon Peak, and the north-east face of Ma On Shan. The rock weathers into smooth rounded surfaces; there is no frost to cleave it into fissures and spikes, and such ledges as exist are usually covered with tough and prickly vegetation. Rock-climbing offers no attractions in Hong Kong, and the cliffs are best avoided when you are out scrambling.

Most of the hills are grass-covered, and in the distance look invitingly smooth to walk over. But if you are rash enough to leave the path, you will find that the grass can by no manner of means be described as springy turf; it is rank and thick, and often conceals an unspeakable surface of rough boulders and scree. Fortunately there are paths almost everywhere on the hills, and you can wander at will, unhindered by game preserves and private property.

The southern slopes, exposed to the full heat of the sun during the dry season, are often bare, and the red ribs of the hills push out from their covering of grass. Here erosion has full play and cuts precipitous gullies and canyons in the soft rock—nasty places to stumble into on a dark night. There are some deep chasms of this sort in the foothills behind Kowloon Tong, where the ruthless cutting of trees and shrubs for firewood has hastened the process of denudation.

The richest vegetation is found on the northern slopes; in the shady hollows the ground retains some moisture even after weeks of drought, and these places are often a paradise of flowering shrubs, of wonderful

parts. Building materials and all sorts of other stuff can be held in depots in the New Territories for a fraction of what it would cost in the city. Until very recently there have been no restrictions on this sort of redevelopment, and landowners have taken advantage of the opportunity to earn much more than they could by farming.

Finally, city dwellers began to remember that there was countryside out there. As they got more leisure time, they started to return to the New Territories and the islands to hold barbecues and picnics, to walk, to sail, and in many other ways to escape from the busy city life. Lord Murray Maclehose, governor from 1971 to 1982, was an enthusiastic advocate of this trend. He was influential in creating the country parks, protected by statute from development and urbanisation.

Whether Graham would have approved of these trends can perhaps be gleaned from a closer look at his life. He was a straightforward and modest man. As Director of the Observatory, he demanded scrupulously high standards of reporting. I can't imagine him falsifying records or fudging results to get a job done. 'The end doesn't justify the means', I could imagine him saying. It's a feature of rambling, too, that the way you get there is as important as where you get to.

Graham also had an adventurous and romantic side, Veronica remembered: 'When my father would drive me back to boarding school, he took the pain out of the journey by pointing out constellations and Andromeda, the only other galaxy that one can see with the naked eye, telling us of how many thousand years the light took to reach us, filling us with wonder at the vast mysteriousness of the universe.' His third quality, humour, was perhaps the most important. His book echoes a rather lighthearted approach to life, a good-natured and even-tempered approach. According to Veronica, 'my father's advice, when under pressure, is to MAINTAIN A SENSE OF HUMOUR AT ALL COSTS!' Finally, Graham cared deeply for the people around him, and spent a lot of time encouraging young people to reach their full potential. Family, friends, and colleagues recall him with affection.

Graham's close relationship with nature began early. He was the only son of a marriage linking two old English families, both with entries in *Debrett's Peerage*. From his birth in 1903, his nature-loving parents gave him the best opportunities an upper-class English family could offer, and Graham was bright enough to benefit. A search of the archives at New College, Oxford, where he did his degree, suggests that he led a contented and well-behaved life as a student.

From his earliest days at school, he kept a book of 'Nature Notes', right up until a few weeks before his death, with comments on everything from birds, weather, walks, and flowers to hay-making, fox-hunting, and horse-fly bites. His association with Dr. Herklots led him to write for and co-edit the *Hong Kong Naturalist*. He was at home on land or water; he rowed for his school, coxed for his college crew

variety and beauty. The contrast between the north and south slopes is strikingly shown on the Hunchback ridge of Ma On Shan, where the thick scrub which covers the north-west face comes to an end abruptly on the summit ridge, as if trimmed by hedge-clippers, and gives place to the rough grass of the sun-baked southern slopes. Since the country became British territory, wide areas on the hillsides have been planted with pine trees; most of these plantations were destroyed during the Japanese occupation, but reafforestation is now being carried out on a big scale. The pine trees resemble Scots firs, and when you are walking amongst them on a cool winter's day, it is hard to realize that you are within the tropics. If you miss the path while rambling over the hills, it is better to keep to the spurs, where the undergrowth is comparatively sparse, and so avoid the dense and almost impenetrable thickets in the hollows.

In the valleys the scene changes completely. Almost all the level ground is cultivated, and years of diligent farming have made it wonderfully fertile. Paddy fields cover the floor of the valleys, and extend up the lower slopes of the hills; the neat little green terraces, following the curves of the hillsides, are a most attractive feature of the landscape. The villages stand among the fields, each with a grove of trees behind it; these groves often contain some splendid old trees, whose deep shade is delightfully cool in summer. It is in the valleys and around the villages that bird life is most abundant. Many of the villages are walled, reminders of less settled times when each village resembled a fortress; the best-known walled towns are Kam Tin, Old Kowloon City, and Shan Ha Wai near Shatin.

The coastline of the Colony is extraordinarily intricate; wherever you walk you are hardly ever out of sight of some inlet of the sea, which is very confusing if you are without a map. The narrow and steep-sided inlets such as Tolo Channel, which are such a feature of the coast, suggest that the land has sunk since the hills and valleys were first carved out by erosion. Like the fjords of Norway they were once dry land. The only low-lying coast in the Colony is in the north-west, along the shores of the Shum Chun estuary and Deep Bay (the latter is mis-named, for it is very shallow).

(he weighed only 9 stone 7 pounds in 1925, and never got any heavier), and owned two boats in Hong Kong, 'Titania' and 'Spindrift'.

The people closest to him, of course, were his parents, wife, and daughters. He was actively involved in St. Andrew's Church, Kowloon, just behind the Observatory. A lifelong passion for the Boy Scout movement led to his receiving the ultimate accolade, the Golden Acorn, from the Queen at Windsor Castle. And he chose his friends to reflect his beliefs; they were all like-minded people with deep interests in developing the community.

When the war came, Graham was interned. The three-and-a-half years in camp must have gone against the grain of everything he believed in. His unpublished account of his experiences leaves his own contribution to camp life unsaid, but ex-internees credit him with keeping up not only his own morale, but helping others as well.

Rambles was an obvious project for him to undertake. After being introduced to mountaineering by his schoolmaster, Robert Irving, founder of the Ice Club in England, Graham had gained experience in Britain and the Alps. As soon as he started walking in Hong Kong, he would have perceived the need for a guidebook to help others. Unlike his other publications, which are scientific and analytical, *Rambles* allowed him to sing out his heart and soul without restraint.

Graham and Valerie left Hong Kong in 1955, and never returned. He died in southern England on 23 January 1985, aged 81. His gravestone is simple; it carries the family crest and motto, and the inscription: 'A Full Life and Full of Service'. I'm sorry not to have known him. I sense that he made the most of his life, lived it to the full, and passed on his interests and passions to others. I hope I do him justice.

Heywood at the Observatory

At the Royal Observatory, Graham had an extended family that must have satisfied him immensely. On the back cover of From Time Ball To Atomic Clock *(Government Information Services, 1983), a history of the Observatory, there is a photo of the staff taken soon after the end of the war. Graham and Valerie are in the middle of the front row; Susan and Veronica are sitting on the floor with their dog.*

Samuel Cheng confirms Graham's warmth. He joined in 1952 as a junior clerk, and was surprised that the director was on the Recruitment Board for such a lowly post. '"It's hard work, and you have to work night shifts," he warned me', says Cheng. 'It was like a small family then, less than 40 of us altogether, including Mr Heywood's own family. He was a very friendly director, easy to work for and kind to the staff. He talked to us juniors a lot, which was unusual. He encouraged us to work hard and

Continued on page 21

You will find beauty in every mile of our coastline, and if you wander away from the roads and the popular bathing beaches you will be well rewarded. You will come to great cliffs with the white surf breaking round their feet, lonely little beaches visited by no one except an occasional fisherman, and harbours where the junk-fleets come in to anchor and sell their catch in the village. These fishing towns are cheerful places, far more alive than the agricultural villages, for the junk people are genial folk and there is an air of bustle and activity in the shops and boat-building yards.

But this book is intended as a guide to walkers, and an interminable discourse on the beauties of the Colony will never get them anywhere, so I will close this chapter with a list of peaks and passes. It includes all peaks over 1,700 feet in height which are worthy to be ranked as separate mountains. There are innumerable passes; I have listed those which provide the best walks.

PEAKS

Tai Mo Shan	3,130	feet
Lan Tau Peak	3,065	,,
Sunset Peak (Lan Tau Island)	2,858	,,
Rocky Top (Lan Tau Island)	2,530	,,
Ma On Shan	2,261	,,
Grassy Hill	2,144	,,
Pat Sin	2,102	,,
Buffalo Hill	1,987	,,
Kowloon Peak	1,971	,,
Castle Peak (Tsing Shan)	1,906	,,
Unnamed peak N. of Pat Heung	1,874	,,
Tai Tan Yang (N.W. of Lam Tsun)	1,841	,,
Victoria Peak	1,770	,,
Needle Hill	1,741	,,
Mount Parker	1,733	,,

study. In those days, we had to spend four weeks as an Observer on Waglan Island every six months. I got meningitis when I was on duty out there and had to be rushed back to Hong Kong for treatment. I remember Mr Heywood came to see me in hospital. He didn't have to do that, because I was so junior, but it was typical of him.'

When Graham joined in 1932, the expansion of international air routes and the consequent demand for better information was forcing the Observatory to employ extra staff. He threw himself into the work, publishing his first technical paper, 'The Upper Winds of Hong Kong', in 1933. It was the first of many, including a 1950 book, Typhoons, now a classic. Says John Peacock, one of his successors as director: *'Like all of us in those days he was proud of the Observatory's historical record and protective of its reputation. He was a stickler for scientific accuracy and honesty, and meticulous in the maintenance of reliable records.'* As a respected world authority on typhoons, he represented Hong Kong at three international conferences.

By 1955, when he retired, the Observatory had been firmly set on a modern course, but Graham felt that he was out of touch with the latest developments. Perhaps he missed the old days as well. In his 23 years, the methods of forecasting and reporting changed enormously. Cheng says: *'He lived in No.1 Quarters in the grounds, and when there was a typhoon, he used to raise and lower the typhoon signals personally. He often went so far as to do the forecasts himself and write his reasoning in the Appreciation Book, which isn't done now.'*

A Handy Guidebook

From a review in the South China Morning Post, *9 December 1938.*

RAMBLES IN HONGKONG, by G. S. P. Heywood. Price $2.

For some years, the growing number of residents who ramble off the beaten track in this Colony have lamented the absence of an intimate guide to the many delightful places which one can visit. Mr. Heywood has now amply met this need, and will earn the gratitude of present residents as well as those who come here in the future and seek the hills and valleys for week-end recreation.

The author is probably Hongkong's most assiduous walker, and an expert hill climber. For several years, during most of the twelvemonth (but particularly the cool and dry season) he has walked wherever legs could go. And he has always had his eyes open for the beauty of the countryside—the beauty and interest of scenery as well as of nature, unspoiled by man and his works: the result is this small book. As Mr. Heywood says, it is far better to give up a week-end

Continued on page 23

PASSES

Lead Mine Pass .... Tai Po to Shing Mun.
Smuggler's Pass .... Shing Mun to Kowloon Reservoir.
Kowloon Pass .... Kowloon Tong to Shatin.
Shatin Pass .... Kowloon City to Shatin.
Grasscutter's Pass .... Kowloon City to Shatin.
Customs Pass .... Kowloon City to Hebe Haven.
Heather Pass .... Tide Cove to Hebe Haven.
Delta Pass .... Tide Cove to Sai Kung.
Turret Pass .... Shatin to Tai Shui Hang.
Sha Lo Tung Pass .... Tai Po to Kwanti.
Chung Mi Pass .... Sha Tau Kok to Bride's Pool.
The Pass between the Lam Tsun and Pat Heung valleys.
Wong Nei Chong Gap ... Happy Valley to Deep Water Bay.
Tai Tam Gap .... Shau Ki Wan to Tai Tam.
The pass between Tung Chung and Tai O, Lantau Island.

Port Shelter from Tate's Cairn

tennis party for the open spaces; where one can escape civilisation and a teeming populace within less than half an hour. He is an advocate of the peace of the mountaintop, and the health to be had from rambling.

One of the advantages of civilisation and development which we must not decry, however, is the increase of transport facilities, so that it is not always necessary to own or have to hire a motor car, in order to be conveyed to the starting points for various delightful walks or climbs. If anyone doubts that these excursions are delightful, let him try one or two— he should be an instant convert. Mr. Heywood wisely leaves his explored regions largely to speak for themselves: he concerns himself chiefly with telling the reader how to get there, but with deft phrases sketches the many attractions which are to be found, or passed on the way. Hardly an expedition in the New Territories which can be attempted is overlooked, and from these main ventures one can, of course, branch off as the mood dictates.

An excellent sketch map is included at the end of the book, and there are several line drawings, as well as full-page photographic plates of beautiful vistas which ramblers will appreciate, and recall in years to come. Several ways of getting to the top of Taimoshan, of Maonshan, into the Lamtsun Valley, and to the hidden waterfall which few people have managed to reach but which is worth travelling a whole day to see, are given; and such places as the Bride's Pool, the old villages of the New Territories, Castle Peak monastery, Lantau, and other spots of interest or scenic beauty, are also included.

There is a briefer reference to some of the principal walks in Hongkong island; but necessarily, the mainland overshadows everything else, for there alone can the wide spaces of the countryside be encountered.

Much helpful advice is included in this handbook, such as the refreshment needed for an outing and the best way to carry it, and the time required for each excursion. Heights of the Colony's principal hilltops are accurately given. Though the author disclaims much knowledge of natural history, there are frequent references to the fascinations of wild flowers, birds, and other nature subjects which can be encountered.

It should be added that the book is intended to be carried, and repeatedly consulted; and it is of a handy size for that purpose. The price places it within the reach, literally, of all pockets, and one can safely predict that scores of local ramblers will in the next few weeks be possessors of well-thumbed copies.

"Rambles in Hongkong" has been printed by the S. C. M. Post, Ltd., where copies may be obtained.—V.J.

CHAPTER III.

TAI MO SHAN.

A traveller approaching Hong Kong by sea on a clear day sees Tai Mo Shan standing proudly above the rest of the mainland hills, obviously the highest mountain in the Colony. When seen from nearer at hand it is difficult to realize that it is nearly as high as Snowdon, for its bulk is so great and its slopes so gentle. The name means "Big Cloud Mountain".

From Shing Mun. This is the easiest way up the mountain, for the first 600 feet of the ascent, as far as the Jubilee Reservoir, can be made by road. The southeast spur of the mountain, up which the climb is made, comes right down to the reservoir at Pineapple Pass dam, where there is a car park. It would probably be easy to climb directly from the dam, but there is no track, and it is better to follow the broad path along the western shore of the lake, crossing the big catchment which comes in from the left, and continuing for a few hundred yards until a small track is found climbing the hillside above. This soon brings you on to the crest of the spur. The summit of the mountain is out of sight; follow a path towards a big shoulder crowned by a conspicuous rock. Though the final slope up to the shoulder leaves you a little breathless, it is the only steep bit of the climb. As you reach the shoulder the summit comes into view at the far end of a gently sloping ridge; the path becomes a little vague here, twisting in and out of a maze of huge boulders, and on a misty day it might be difficult to follow. But in fine weather it is a grand place, for you are on a high ridge, 2,000 feet up, with splendid views on either side. The path re-appears on a grassy saddle just below the final rise, and the last few hundred feet up to the top are not so exhausting as they look from below. You subside at last, panting, by the summit cairn; the effort was worth while; the whole Colony lies beneath you, and you feel that the worries of civilization have been left a very long way below. The ascent takes about 1¾ hours from the reservoir to the highest point (3,130 feet).

Commentary—Chapter 3

THE military fenced off and levelled the summit of Tai Mo Shan some years ago. Notices on the fence warn that if you do not stop when challenged, you are liable to be shot. Although Graham is not alone in translating the name as Big Cloud Mountain, the Chinese characters used today actually mean Big Hat Mountain; both versions hint at the usual weather conditions.

The route from Shing Mun is still passable all the way except at the top, where it's vanished under the road from Route Twisk. It's quite tricky to find now. You can drive, or take a minibus or taxi up to Pineapple Dam, but it's no longer easier to climb direct from there. After a few minutes in the Visitor Centre, continue up the steps to the right and walk alongside the reservoir until you cross a big catchment on your left. A few yards beyond is a track going up to the road through a BBQ site. Above the road, there are several path junctions among the trees—keep going up. After an open stretch on the ridge, the main path tries to tempt you over to Lead Mine Pass, so stay alert. Just inside the next lot of trees (grid reference 050797), you need to turn off along a tiny unmarked track to your left. After fifty yards or so, turn right at the top of the spur and follow an even fainter track towards the big shoulder.

There aren't any tracks up the shoulder; just make your own. Once you get onto the ridge, you should be able to find a path which goes to the left of the biggest rocky lump on the ridge. Fork right to reach the col, the pass between two hills, beyond the lump (042805). From there, the path heads off to the right up the slope, going between wartime dugouts at the top. When you get to the path below the road (038808) you have three choices— left (stroll up the road), right (scramble up the pipe behind the hut), or straight ahead (thrash through the long grass). Graham went straight ahead, with a clear path to follow.

Whichever choice you make, your final approach is along the road. Scramble around the fence for the full magnificent view which, when the air is really clear, includes mountains in China half-way to Guangzhou. Below us, Hong Kong looks like a miniature.

The first part of the walk from Tai Po by Lead Mine Pass is now a road up to Lo Lau Uk, accessible by minibus from Tai Po. The sign-posted track to Lead Mine Pass starts at the end of the road; it's been 'improved' by the addition of steps, which always seems to me to be the opposite of improvement—I find long flights of steps very tiring.

The path from Lead Mine Pass to the summit is now part of the Maclehose Trail, so tens of thousands of people use it every year. The 'steep slope of 800 feet' from the little gap that Graham mentions has been made easier (or harder?) by the addition of tarmac; from the gap to the top you walk on the other end of the road that starts at Route Twisk.

There are alternatives to the direct route. The first is a track sign-posted 'San Uk Ha', which heads up the

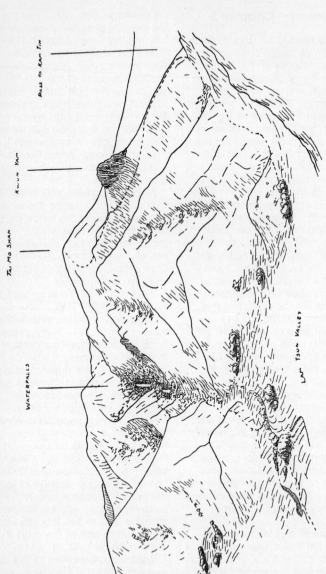

PASS TO KAM TIN

KWUN YAM

TAI MO SHAN

WATERFALLS

LAM TSUN VALLEY

Tai Mo Shan from the North

COMMENTARY

Tea Terraces on Tai Mo Shan

The terraces on Tai Mo Shan are generally supposed to be the remains of tea cultivation. The 1688 District Gazetteer refers to them in this translation by James Hayes from his book, The Rural Communities of Hong Kong: *'Tai Mo Shan is 50 Chinese miles east of the District City. It has the shape of a big hat. It extends south and west from Ng Tung Mountain. Its peak measures 2,000 Chinese feet. It is a big mountain in the fifth Division, with a stone pagoda and many tea plantations.'*

The Rev R. Krone visited this area in 1858. Here is his account, as reprinted in the 1984 JHKBRAS: 'Tea is also cultivated in several places and is generally called 'Shan-cha' (mountain tea). It has a rather strong astringent taste, but is much liked by the natives, and particularly by those who are of advanced age, who consider that it promotes digestion and cools the system. Many drink only this indigenous tea.'

According to the same volume, the Hui family of Lo Wai village, above Tsuen Wan, used to collect tea from wild bushes near the summit of Tai Mo Shan.

One old man, born in 1896, used to collect ten catties a week during the season, commenting that the best time for plucking the leaves was in the third lunar month. This type of tea was described as 'wan mo' ('cloud mist'). He began doing this when he was about ten years old, selling to other villagers and not to shops or teahouses. He also collected medicinal herbs on the mountain. Another favourable location for wild tea trees, he said, was Nam Tong To where the Shing Mun villagers collected.

A notice erected by Kadoorie Farm at Kwun Yam Shan, however, says that the terraces may be much older:

The rock terrace on the mountain-sides . . . said to have been constructed for tea-bush growing about two hundred years ago. There are reasons to believe they are far older, and that they were constructed for crop-growing in times of famine and civil war, or by migrant peoples or refugees who had been rejected as settlers by the local inhabitants.

From Tai Po by Lead Mine Pass. A longer but more varied route than that described above. Leaving Tai Po Market the path goes under the railway bridge about 200 yards east of the station, crosses the stream and follows it, first on its east side and then on its west, all the way up a pleasant valley to Lead Mine Pass. From the pass a faint track diverges to the right on to a high plateau and there loses itself in the long grass. There *may* be a continuous track from the pass to the summit, but I have never discovered it. From the grassy plateau a way is forced with toil and tribulation up two or three hundred feet of hillside to the crest of the mountain's north-east ridge. Large areas of this part of the mountain are fired nearly every winter; on one occasion we had to dodge through the line of burning grass, and were able to watch a number of Kestrels hovering over the flames, on the look-out for unfortunate reptiles and grasshoppers driven from cover by the heat. These fires are said to be started deliberately, for the ash, when washed down by the rain, benefits the paddy fields below. Shrubs and young trees suffer severely, but the grass roots are undamaged and by the following summer the hillside is green again.

On the ridge another path is picked up, which wanders inconsequently in and out of the hummocks, now and then disappearing for a few yards among the boulders. This ridge can also be reached from the north by a side valley which comes down to the Lead Mine stream at the village of Yuen Tun Ha, about a mile and a half south of Tai Po; this is a good variation of the ordinary route via Lead Mine Pass. Continuing along the ridge, the path dips to a little gap, and finally climbs the last steep slope of 800 feet to the summit. Time from Tai Po, 3¾ hours. The traverse of Tai Mo Shan from Tai Po to Shing Mun or Tsun Wan is a fine expedition for a long day's outing.

From the Lam Tsun Valley. Tai Mo Shan hides its greatest charms on its northern face, overlooking the upper end of the Lam Tsun valley. If you are a bird-lover, you will seldom get to the foot of the mountain on this side, for there is so much to see in the woods lower down. Only by leaving your field glasses at home, and firmly refusing to be lured off the path by any birds, charm they never so sweetly, can you hope

hillside to your right just before the Lo Lau Uk road crosses the stream (077835), and reaches a 588-metre top high up on the ridge. On the map, the main path contours round to the east from there and joins the Maclehose Trail. I've tried but failed to follow this path, only managing to reach the ridge after scrambling through the bushes. It might be better to follow the smaller path that goes straight up the ridge to the south from 054828.

Another alternative is the paved path to Ta Tit Yan. From the tidy Kwun Yam Temple behind the village, a path disappears into the trees. It looks OK there, and it looks OK from the road above, but I don't know about the bit in the middle; it's on my 'next winter' list.

Graham's Yuen Tun Ha variation probably doesn't go now. Above the village, one path goes to the stream, where pipes collect fresh water. The other path veers left and climbs under the trees past a deserted temple, only to get overgrown and greasy as it emerges in the open. On a hot summer day, I abandoned it after a hundred yards. Another for 'next winter', but low on the list.

A road has replaced the path in the centre of the Lam Tsun Valley, and progress has come to Lam Tsuen (as it's now spelt). Although it's brought economic gain to the people who live here, it's a bit of a loss to the weekend rambler searching for rural tranquillity. Away from the road, though, birds still sing in the woods, and I'm told by birdwatching friends that this is a sweet place to be charmed. The stream, protected by regulations

against farm waste, runs as clean as any in Hong Kong.

Graham's 'substantial old bridge' proved as insubstantial as so much else, unfortunately, and so stopped getting older. You can still walk to the pass, of course, so long as you don't mind walking with buses, taxis, and trucks belting past within inches. Exploring the side paths of the valley is an interesting way to spend an afternoon.

Kadoorie Farm has commandeered the hillside south of the pass. The only way now to get up the ridge below Kwun Yam Shan is through the farm, and to get into the farm you'll need a permit. (If you use this as a descent route, you don't need a permit to get out.) They've rearranged the landscape so if you want to climb their hill, you'll have to use their roads. Phone 488-1317 a few days in advance for a permit, and take a leisurely stroll up through the Farm. Feast your eyes on the seasonal delights on display. Kwun Yam Shan has honeysuckle, and notices explaining 'ancient altars' and 'hot pots'. The hill opposite has an international signpost (samples— Macau: 35 miles, Bombay: 2,678 miles, Los Angeles: 7,230 miles, Rio de Janeiro: 10,992 miles), and a relief model of Hong Kong which interprets physical reality very creatively.

The way to the summit starts at the Kwun Yam Shan col. Go through the T.S. Woo Pavilion and up to the covered reservoir. If you can't find a clear way straight ahead over the spur, turn right through the gate, and go along the path leading to the Farm's water supply for a hundred metres or so,

to get through the Lam Tsun valley in reasonable time. But a description of this delightful place must be deferred to another chapter.

On the left of the Fanling road, about a mile and a quarter from Tai Po Market, is a substantial old bridge over a stream. This is the entrance to the Lam Tsun valley; a walk of rather over an hour along the main path through the valley will bring you to the low pass at its head. This way is far preferable to the approach to the pass from Yuen Long and Kam Tin on the far side, which entails a long walk through the somewhat flat and uninteresting Pat Heung valley.

About a hundred yards below the pass on the Lam Tsun side, a grasscutters' track (shown on the accompanying sketch) diverges to the left and takes you up the steep grass of the ridge towards an imposing rocky spur, which stands above the pass. This spur is named after Kwun Yam, the Buddhist Goddess of Mercy; a most appropriate name, for the hill seems to give its blessing to the two most fertile valleys in the Colony, which lie at its feet. At the foot of the rocks, about 500 feet above the pass, the track is joined by another path, which comes direct up the hillside from the nunnery at the head of the Pat Heung valley. From here the path traverses across the hillside under the north face of Kwun Yam to a point just below the saddle connecting the spur with the mountain; leave the main path and clamber up a smaller track for a few yards on to the saddle behind Kwun Yam. It is worth dumping your haversack here, and scrambling over the tumbled rocks to the top of the spur, for it is a fine viewpoint and it will only take you ten minutes to get there; flowering shrubs grow in profusion between the rocks, and here and there a rhododendron makes a gorgeous splash of colour.

From the saddle the track continues up the ridge all the way to the summit of Tai Mo Shan, reached in about 2 hours from the pass at the head of the Lam Tsun valley. The upper slopes are terraced by rough stone walls, the origin of which is something of a mystery; perhaps they were made by grass-cutters to clear the ground of rocks and to prevent the soil being carried down by erosion; or they may be the terraces of disused tea plantations.

Photo. G. A. C. Herklots

The Gateway of Romance, Lam Tsun Valley

From Tsun Wan. Before the construction of the road up to Shing Mun reservoir, the ascent of Tai Mo Shan was usually made from the village of Tsun Wan, which lies to the south of the mountain on the Castle Peak road. The path started just beyond the bridge where the road crosses the stream running through the village, about 8¼ miles from Kowloon. The crest of the south ridge was followed all the way to the summit—a long and rather uninteresting slog up a barren hillside. The ascent took about 2½ hours. The Japanese built a road up the mountain from Tsun Wan; this has now fallen into disuse.

The long plod up the south ridge of Tai Mo Shan, so wearisome in broad daylight, becomes an enchanted pilgrimage under the full moon. One bright night a large party of us spent 5½ hours in making the ascent— probably a record for slowness, but there was every reason not to hurry, and as our cavalcade zig-zagged leisurely up the path one could almost recapture the thrill of a midnight start for a big peak in the Alps. We halted half way up, lit a bonfire and brewed cocoa, which tasted better than it has ever done before or since; as we lay back and watched the distant lights of Hong Kong we did not envy in the least the people lying snugly abed in the town. From the summit we saw the sunrise; such moments cannot be described, but none of us is likely to forget them.

Tsun Wan has several local industries; silk-weaving is carried on in an up-to-date mill next door to the primitive and unhygienic sheds where noodles are made from powdered beans. In the valley running up into the hills to the south-west of Tai Mo Shan there is a village consisting entirely of watermills, where wood is ground up for the manufacture of joss sticks. This picturesque place is easily reached from the road; the path starts at the bridge about half a mile beyond Tsun Wan, near the 9th milestone, and follows the stream upwards, first on one bank and then on the other. The first water-mill is reached in 5 minutes' walk from the road, and beyond are a dozen more little houses perched on the sides of the valley, each with its waterwheel busily turning. For a small tip the owner of one of these mills will show your inside; the atmosphere is thick with fragrant dust, and through it you can dimly see great stone-headed hammers pounding away at the aromatic wood.

and find a way up to the ridge on your left. Stay on the ridge all the way to the road at the top.

Although Graham refers to a path down to the nunnery at Ling Wan Tsz, and a path is shown on the map, I doubt if it's a passable route now.

The village at the start of the walk from Tsun Wan (now spelt Tsuen Wan) has been completely swallowed by a new town of the same name. A dozen other villages have disappeared too, but one (Sam Tung Uk) was kept and made into a museum—the opposite of renovation. It's worth a visit. The permanent display is supplemented by periodic exhibitions showing aspects of traditional Hong Kong life such as rice farming, architecture, and paper kites.

The south ridge is quite interesting. Inspired by Graham's midnight ramble, I took a small party of friends up this way one December night. A few obvious diversions were necessary at the start, where you can't follow the old route exactly, but from the ridge at 030784, it's pretty clear. Taking my cue from accounts of earlier ascents, I had asked the Regional Services Department for advice on hiring mules and coolies, but they were unable to assist.

We left Tsuen Wan MTR at 11.30, and pottered slowly up, resting frequently, chatting, and admiring the unfolding views of the city lights. We reached the top at 5.00 and saw a memorable dawn at 6.30. The sun rose and went behind a low bank of cloud above the horizon, from where it seemed to rise again a few minutes later; that was the only cloud in the sky that day. As we walked down to Route Twisk to the bus, my friends, none of whom had ever walked at night, agreed that it had been an enchanted pilgrimage.

The old Japanese road was actually built by British POWs from the Argyle Street Officers' Camp. You can still walk it all the way, although only on one section can you see the original surface. It formed the start of Route Twisk as far as Chuen Lung Village. From there, it's now the minor road giving access to the cemetery. To the north of the cemetery, the wartime surface is still visible in a zigzag section which ends up at the Sze Lok Yuen Youth Hostel—a section which is now passable only by pedestrians. From there to the summit, the new road follows the old road.

Many people nowadays climb Tai Mo Shan from Route Twisk. This approach has the added advantage that you can drive all the way to the Tai Mo Shan Road barrier at 700 metres, leaving less than 300 metres to climb. If you feel lazy, you can just sit in your car and enjoy the view. If you feel energetic, try the direct path which cuts out all the zigzags on the road, and comes out by the fence at the top. There's a handy flat rock half way up for a breather. This is a bad descent route; it's greasy underfoot, so you need to see where you're treading, but it's so overgrown that you can't, and the combination makes it dangerous.

Although I think it's a pity that more people don't try alternative routes, I suppose it has an

There are some good bathing-pools in this valley, though in dry weather most of the water from the stream is diverted through the mills.

The Waterfalls. When coming home from Fanling by road, you can see on a clear day a streak of silver high up in a corrie on the distant northerly face of Tai Mo Shan. This is the upper part of a really splendid waterfall, whose existence is probably known to few walkers, as from close at hand it is hidden by lower spurs. The gorge and its waterfalls are almost inaccessible from below, but it is possible for a determined party to reach them from above; with the help of 30 feet of rope, it is then possible to climb down the gorge beneath the falls, and so descend into the Lam Tsun valley. I do not want to lure any walkers into places where they would much rather not be, so I must say at once that the descent involves some complicated route-finding, a scramble down steep scree in thick jungle, and a bit of gymnastics on waterworn rocks. It is worth it, though; the gorge is a most entrancing place. To be on the safe side, allow 3 hours of daylight for descending the mountain by this route; the way is difficult to find, and you may have to retrace your steps and reach the valley by a more orthodox path.

The waterfall stream rises immediately to the north of the little pass which can be seen in the accompanying sketch to the left of the summit of Tai Mo Shan. This point may be reached by following the Lead Mine Pass route along the ridge as far as the gap about half a mile north-east of the summit and a few hundred feet below it. A quicker way is to go up the Lam Tsun valley, and take the path, already described, which leads to Kwun Yam. Instead of climbing up to the saddle behind Kwun Yam, continue along the path, which winds in and out of the gullies high up on the hillside, climbing gradually all the time. Eventually you come round to the head of the waterfall valley, reached in about 2¼ hours from the Fanling road. Before you reach the source of the stream, a faint track will be found going steeply down on your left into the upper part of the gorge. The track follows a grassy spur for a couple of hundred feet down to the stream, which it crosses. Here, amongst the trees, is a lovely little pool, so secret and hidden away that water nymphs must surely come and dance around it on moonlit nights. On

advantage for those who like to be alone. If you walk the south ridge, or go up from Pineapple Dam, I promise you won't meet anyone at all (if you do, ask them if they've read this book).

The Waterfalls: And now to one of Graham's favourite places, the Ng Tung Chai Waterfalls. There are four of them and they are a well-kept secret. It was only Graham's book that alerted me to them in the first place, and it was only very recently that I discovered the fourth fall and the water nymphs' pool. A rope is not needed nowadays—a good track will take you there from either above or below. The falls are visited rarely and they're gems, especially after rain.

From above, there's a superb modern path along which an army could march. It has eliminated route-finding complications, scrambles down jungly scree, and gymnastics on waterworn rocks, although you might lament the sacrifice of the mystery. I notice that the path goes through a ruined house just above the falls, which makes me wonder whether the banana trees were wild or planted.

But who would have lived all the way up here?

Approaching from below, you can catch a minibus from Tai Po, which turns round on the main road just below Ng Tung Chai village. One of the Tai Po-Ng Tung Chai minibus drivers is Indonesian, recognisable by the wispy hairs on his chin. He's been in Hong Kong for 10 years with little chance to use his English, and he loves to talk. As you climb above the village, there are tantalising glimpses of the main fall. It looks a long way away, and in fact I'm always surprised by the time it takes to get up there. You need to be careful, too; the steps may be slippery if it's been raining. This north-facing valley is often damp when the rest of Hong Kong is dry.

Allow at least four hours to visit all four falls, take photos, paddle, or bathe, and return to the road. Don't let darkness overtake you on your descent—the light fades early in here. I prefer to walk up: each waterfall is then bigger than the one before, and makes more of an impression. And the secret pool is such a refreshing end to the climb.

the far side of the stream the track traverses the open hillside for a short distance; on your left is empty space, for you are close above the big waterfall, though it is still out of sight. Before long you come to a gully, filled with scree and thickly wooded; turn straight down this, being careful not to plunge headlong over the cliff at its lower end. The track is now visible only to the eye of faith; a detour can be made to the right, avoiding the cliff, through a jungle of wild banana trees to the stream-bed below. It is a fascinating place for a botanist; orchids and tree-ferns grow in abundance in the damp atmosphere of the gorge, and, by way of contrast, there is a little creeping bramble, whose delicate white flowers bring memories of an English heath.

A few yards more and you have reached the object of your quest. You are shut in by the steep sides of the gorge; a dark cliff rises in front of you, and over its edge, 150 feet above your head, the stream sparkles in the light and falls in one cascade to a clear pool among the rhododendrons at your feet. Yes, your toils are rewarded.

Perhaps a hundred yards below the big fall is a smaller one, and it is here that the rope comes in useful. The sides of the gorge are vertical and quite impracticable, and the only way of escape is to rope down the little cliff by the side of the fall and wade the pool 40 feet below. Fortunately there is a small but tough tree-stump at the edge of the cliff; the rope is looped round this, and the party descends hand over hand in more or less undignified attitudes. It is as well to send the heaviest man down last, for then if the stump gives way under his weight the party will quickly be re-united. It is not really an alarming place, for though the rock is smooth and holdless it slopes away at a fairly easy angle.

The difficulties are now nearly over; after a few hundred yards of boulder-hopping down the bed of the stream, a track can be found on the right bank, opposite the point where a small tributary joins the main stream from the west. This path crosses the open hillside to the east of the gorge, above the lower of the two big waterfalls. From here there should be no trouble in following the path down to the Lam Tsun

COMMENTARY

Previous Ascents of Tai Mo Shan

Tai Mo Shan has long been a popular destination. Two charming accounts of nineteenth century excursions are in print. The first is the story of an 1859 trip reprinted in Hong Kong Illustrated: Views and News 1840–1890 *(John Warner Publications, 1981):*

Those who are accustomed to travel by rail in cushioned carriages, with a hotel and other luxuries waiting for them at their journey's end, will be astonished to see the style of vehicle in which we perform our voyages of discovery—a frail bamboo chair supported by two lusty coolies, with two more to relieve them when blown.

The second account, from The Hong Kong Guide 1893 *(Oxford University Press, 1982), contains advice for 'the excursion . . . which may be regarded as the pilgrimage to Mecca for all faithful pedestrians':*

There is only one way to the summit, but as no two members of the Hongkong Alpine Club agree upon which way that is, it is as well not to go into details about it, especially as they would be wholly useless. One may possibly be allowed to mention his modest but unalterable conviction that his way is *the* way, and that there is no other, and his utter scepticism as to statements about a path 'almost to the top,' unless almost means at least, six or seven hundred feet. And that last pull is, it must be confessed, a very stiff one, whether the grass be long and thus hide all the big stones, or whether it has just been burned, and so all the ground be slippery with black ashes which rise up and choke you. . . . An Alpen-stock is useful on this walk, and so are neutral tinted goggles, a pair of which is an immense comfort on any midday excursion. A few rare ferns are found near the top of Tai-mo Shan, of which one has never been discovered elsewhere except in Java.

An 1896 publication, Tourists' Map of 8 Short Trips on the Mainland of China (neighbourhood of Hong Kong), including The Principal Places Frequented by Sportsmen, With Vocabulary in Cantonese and Hakka, *by R. C. Hurley, advised the traveller to Tai Mo Shan that 'It is a good plan to hire a village lad as a guide, who will also assist in carrying the tiffin basket, always keeping him on ahead.' Hurley's preparations for walks included:*

Passports (always useful) procurable in Canton: and the national flag of the party. *Boat.* Steam-launch and, or, Hakka boat with a small punt or dingy. *Wardrobe.* Seasonable, according to duration of trip (sun topey indispensible). *Commissariat.* Fresh water, fresh meat, pies, bread, potatoes, salt, tinned meats, butter, milk and preserves, tea, coffee, sugar, and a cruet. *Light.* Oil lamps, candles, matches. *Sporting gear.* Fowling piece, duck gun, and revolver, with ammunition for all. *Recreation.* Cards, reading matter, cigars, and tobacco. *Personal.* Medicines and Liquors. *Pocket Compass and pedometer.*

Continued on page 39

valley. The dusk is falling as you step out along the homeward path; a good day on the hills is behind you, and a hot bath and supper in front; what more could one wish? And never mind *how* dishevelled you are when you board the train at Tai Po.

Waterwheel

COMMENTARY

In The Hong Kong Countryside *(South China Morning Post Ltd., 1951), Dr G. A. C. Herklots described a walk, very similar to Graham's midnight ramble, on which they may have been companions:*

Some years before the war, with the co-operation of H. M. Navy, a moonlight climb of Tai Mo Shan was arranged for 24th October. By launch and bus a dozen of us proceeded to Tsun Wan from where our climb was to start; there we were joined by a cavalcade of mules laden with wood and water, food and blankets. It was a perfect night for the climb and the moon gave sufficient light for us to see the path clearly. Needless to say the leaders went off the track and had to retrace their steps to join the rest of the party behind the mules. One mule sideslipped and sat on a roll of bedding and also, as subsequent examination proved, on my tube of tooth paste. Disliking the smell of mules I took a short cut to regain the van of the expedition and disturbed a snake whose loud hiss caused me to jump aside and to make a slight detour.

The mules found difficulty in ascending the last steep slope so we camped some 500 feet below the summit. Some of us, at about 11.45 p.m. made a brief trip to the top of the mountain, 3130 feet, whilst the others lit a huge fire. A colossal meal was followed by a sing-song round the camp fire. There were no chestnuts to roast but I speared an apple on a stick and propped it up in front of the blaze. Some were envious of my idea, but they were gratified and amused when the apple on being opened was found to be the tomb of a roasted maggot. A second apple fortunately proved to be uninhabited. Out with the blankets and soon we were asleep.

Long before dawn enthusiastic sun worshippers were calling on the rest to hasten if they wished to see the sunrise from the top of the mountain. Never have I dressed so quickly, if taking off a second pair of flannel trousers and putting on a pair of shoes can be called dressing! Soon we were scrambling up the last ascent, puffing and panting and stumbling over rocks, for the moon had long since set, in our haste to see the sun. Alas, a bank of cloud in the east hid the rising sun and it was quite light before the red globe appeared above the cloud. Back to the camp fire where we ate a sumptuous breakfast. The blankets having been packed and the mules laden we said goodbye to the Indian gunners and Chinese boys and set off once more for the mountain top. Here we divided into two parties; the lazybones including the ladies set off for Fanling. . . . The five more energetic males laden with a rope, food and towels descended to a precipitous ravine. . . .

Presently we came to a waterfall 100 feet high, one of the finest in the Territories; this necessitated a detour. Further down we arrived at a precipice at the foot of which was a deep pool. I attempted to climb round and down to the pool, and whilst doing this my basket containing rare orchids, a clean shirt, and my lunch fell and bounced from rock to rock until it arrived with a splash in the water. The detour proved to be impossible. Each in turn descended with the aid of the rope to a ledge of rock immediately above the pool. Here we undressed and flung our clothes across the pool and nude slid down into the icy but refreshing water.

Another waterfall lower down was impassable so we left this ravine and followed a grass-cutters' path which took us to a stream in the next valley. Here we bathed and sunned ourselves on the rocks and ate our lunch, which in my case consisted of a sodden pork pie and a bruised apple. Suddenly a snake emerged from behind a stone; we kept still and watched it work its way up stream looking behind rocks and roots in search of a frog. It passed over my blazer and disappeared amongst the undergrowth on a bank above.

CHAPTER IV.

THE KOWLOON HILLS AND SHATIN.

Kowloon means "Nine Dragons"; the name is supposed to refer to the line of hills which encloses the town on the north, but whichever way I count them I have never been able to make them add up to nine. The streets of Kowloon for the most part are, I fear, terribly commonplace and ugly, and these fine hills standing up behind the houses are the only things which save the town from complete mediocrity.

The new roads over the Kowloon hills have made great scars on the hillsides, but they are superb pieces of engineering. In a quarter of an hour or so from the town you can motor up to a height of 1,700 feet; to drive a powerful car up one of these wonderful roads must be a sensation as near flying as you can get on solid earth. I know of no better drive to take a visitor who has only a few hours to spend in Hong Kong, for from the highest point on the road you can see over practically the whole of the Colony.

The Kowloon range, running from Kowloon Reservoir to Customs Pass, is too well known to walkers to need much description; a few walks within easy reach of the town will be mentioned.

Around Kowloon Reservoir at the western end of the range there are several good paths which afford pleasant strolls for a summer evening. A branch of the Tai Po road crosses the dam below the reservoir, and winds upwards towards Golden Hill on the far side. Not far from the dam a flight of steps will be found on the left, leading to an upper lake with a path encircling it. There is also a good path beside the catchwater on the other side of the Tai Po road; this flows for several miles along the northern slopes of the Kowloon hills, and enters the reservoir at the bridge where the fishermen stand. The path is perfectly flat, and would make a good "invalids' walk."

In the pinewoods between the reservoir and Lai Chi Kok I once came across an enormous swarm of butterflies; there must have been many thousands of them crowding on the bushes and flitting about amongst

Commentary—Chapter 4

MANY people, including me, have tried and failed to count nine hills. But there is a story about the last Song dynasty emperor who fled from the invading Mongols in the twelfth century. He landed on the Kowloon peninsula near what is now Kai Tak airport, which wasn't there then, of course. The emperor, who was often likened to the dragon, most powerful of animals, was told that the place was called Eight Dragons because there were eight hills on the peninsula. One of his aides quipped that there was now an extra dragon, referring to the emperor, so it should be called 'Nine Dragons'. So the name refers to the hills on the peninsula, not to the range behind. Most of them are gone now, demolished to make way for a city that is more than ever enhanced by the hills behind.

The Kowloon Reservoirs are popular for recreation. Macaque monkeys live in the woods beside the catchwater path. They were common in the nineteenth century, but died out in the early 1900s and reappeared only in the 1960s; that's why Graham doesn't mention them. Strolling along here one day, I was threatened by a group of six or seven; I growled and stared at them and scared them a bit, but I've since learned that staring, far from frightening them, is regarded as a challenge. Butterfly Valley is now recognised by its own name on the map. The hills are green again—and the descendants of Graham's butterflies are still fluttering by.

Most of the walks described by Graham on this range can still be followed. However, extensive post-war urban development means that adjustments will be necessary for some of the approaches. The walks over the passes offer some surprises and, as Graham notes, can be done in half a day, making them ideal introductions to the hills.

Kowloon Pass (094745) is no longer named as such on the map, and if you try to ask at the Kowloon Walled City for the path up to Kowloon Pass, you will get some pretty odd looks. Actually, the old Walled City probably won't exist by the time you're reading this. It's going to be made into a park, with the old 'yamen' building, or fort, in the middle as a museum. The wall which used to surround it was carted off during the war by the Shamshuipo POWs (possibly Graham among them) to build the foundation for a longer runway at Kai Tak. There's a good account of its history in *Forts and Pirates*, published in 1990 by the Hong Kong History Society.

The paths up to Kowloon Pass from the south are hard to find, so I recommend that you do it from the Sha Tin side, and then you can grab a cab wherever you come down on the Kowloon side. One way is to walk along the catchwater from the west to 091752 and up the minor footpath on the map, which is actually part of the old Imperial Road. Lion Rock is glimpsed from the catchwater, and then suddenly looms overhead when you emerge from the trees below the pass. It looks irresistible, especially on a sunny afternoon. Another approach to the pass is to

the trees. What brought them there I do not know; they did not seem to be feeding or laying eggs, and there was no sign of empty chrysalises. The pinewoods around the reservoir alas disappeared during the war, but the slopes are greening over once more with scrub and bamboo.

The three main passes over the range are crossed by excellent paths, any one of which provides a good half-day's walk from Kowloon over to Shatin, whence the return can be made by train. The most westerly of the three gaps in the range is **Kowloon Pass** (1,036 feet), between Beacon Hill and Lion Rock. The path starts in a roundabout way near the old walled city of Kowloon, but the pass may be reached more directly from the bus stop in Kowloon Tong at the top end of Waterloo Road. A little valley will be found opening on the north-east corner of the large area of level ground on the right of the road. A short scramble up the bank on the east of this valley will bring you on to a low ridge where you strike the main path up to the pass. The hillsides overlooking the town have been ruthlessly stripped of timber, and ugly patches of bare red earth are taking the place of shady groves. But the northern slopes on the far side of the pass are greener, and here you may find a wealth of flowering shrubs. From the pass the track goes straight down a valley, crossing the catchwater and reaching the paddy fields to the south of Shatin not far from the mouth of the railway tunnel.

Shatin Pass (963 feet), which lies between Lion Rock and Temple Hill, is the lowest pass over the range. It can be reached by a steep and narrow by-road, practicable for cars, which leaves the main-road on the north side of Kai Tak airport just beyond the runway crossing. A pleasanter and more direct way is to take a lane which branches off to the right fifty yards from the main-road, and follow it for about half a mile to a point a few yards short of a dairy farm. Here a path diverges to the left and leads upwards to a little temple perched picturesquely on the steep slope of the hill to which it gives its name. The keepers of the temple will provide you with tea, which they produce from the ubiquitous thermos flask.

The Old Imperial Road

Hong Kong's communications with the centre of the Chinese Empire, more than a thousand miles to the north, were slow and hazardous before modern air travel. The Empire's local outpost was the yamen in the middle of Kowloon Walled City, manned by a few hundred troops. An envoy sent by the commander of this fort with an urgent message for Beijing could go two ways: by sea, or overland.

The sea traveller embarked a few hundred yards southeast, at a jetty where Kai Tak Airport Terminal now stands; photos of the Walled City from the jetty will be on display when the yamen reopens as a museum. The sea voyage was much quicker than going overland, but the pirates made it risky.

So travellers often went by road, hoping they wouldn't be attacked by bandits. From the fort, a paved footpath led northwest, over Kowloon Pass to the west of Lion Rock, and down to Sha Tin. A boat took them through Tide Cove and Tolo Harbour, and into the inlet that is now the northern arm of Plover Cove Reservoir. Landing at Chung Mei, they followed another paved footpath upstream to Wu Kau Tang, north over the hills, and reached the coast again at Tai Wan. Here they took a second boat trip, across Starling Inlet to Sha Tau Kok before joining the main coast road going north-east. That was the first day; sixty more lay ahead.

The 1898 treaty which leased the New Territories to Great Britain for ninety-nine years fudged the issue of jurisdiction over the Walled City. The Chinese thought they could continue to station soldiers there, and believed they retained a right of way along this route in order to communicate with the yamen. In late 1990 an illegal immigrant being sent back to China successfully appealed against his deportation order, claiming that he had in fact entered Hong Kong via this route and was thus a perfectly legal immigrant. If I had been the magistrate, I would have invited him for a walk to show me exactly how he had come.

From here it is a climb of only five minutes to the pass, on which stands a ruined bungalow. The path follows a stream down a long straight valley on the far side of the pass, bringing you out eventually near the walled village of Shan Ha Wai to the east of Shatin. Some attractive frescos adorn the archways leading into this village.

The Temple, Shatin Pass

The third and most easterly of the three passes is **Grasscutter's** (1,300 feet). From Kai Tak, take the route described above as far as the dairy farm at the foot of the hill. Here a paved path, not very easily noticed, branches off to the left of the lane between the dairy farm buildings, and leads up the hillside to the pass. The latter can also be reached by a continuation of the Shatin Pass road. On the far side the path bears away to the right, coming down through a beautiful wooded valley past tiny villages set in orange groves, and ending on the shore of Tide Cove about two miles from Shatin.

So much for the passes. The peaks need little description for there is a path along the whole skyline of the range, and any of the summits can be reached without difficulty from the passes on either side.

Beacon Hill and **Lion Rock** (1,618 feet) are most easily climbed from Kowloon Pass which crosses the gap between them. Lion Rock is a great feature in the view from the town or the harbour, and it is a fine mountain, for all that its head is less than 2,000 feet

start from Hung Mui Kuk village in Sha Tin and visit Amah Rock on the way.

It's easiest to approach the Kwun Yam temple below Sha Tin Pass from behind the Tsz Wan Shan bus terminus. A plaque in the temple records that it was built in 1853 by religious merchants who used the road at the foot of the hill. Devotees and incense smoke fill the normally deserted temple for Kwun Yam ceremonies on the 19th day of the 2nd, 6th, 9th, and 11th Chinese months. The Chinese name for Temple Hill, to the east of the pass, is Merciful Cloud Hill.

Below here is the large Wong Tai Sin temple, which is filled 365 days a year. Wong Tai Sin's autobiography is on the altar. As explained by Joyce Savidge in *This is Hong Kong: Temples* (Government Information Services, 1977):

The god tells how he was originally a shepherd boy, guarding his flock in a remote area of China's Chekiang province, on Red Pine Hill. At 15, he was blessed by an immortal who took him to a cave where he learned the art of refining cinnabar into an immortal drug. He then spent 40 years in seclusion until he was tracked down by his brother, who wanted to know what had happened to the sheep. Wong Tai Sin took his brother to a spot that was full of white boulders, which he straightway transformed into sheep.

Shan Ha Wai is at the lower end of the valley to the north, a few hundred yards to the west. The village, also called Tsang Tai Uk, is worth a visit. A family member used to own a quarry on Hong Kong Island; his business boomed after the British came and he built this substantial village with his profits. The tridents on the corner towers stop evil spirits from sitting down and bringing bad luck.

The old paths leading up to Grasscutter's Pass from the Kowloon side are unused and overgrown. North of the pass, a network of roads serves a sizeable community of farmers and squatters. One of these roads, the central one, goes down to Tso Tui Ha where there's a villa estate built some years ago in expectation of a road link to Sha Tin. But because of the country park, the government decided not to build a road. Local villagers, finally despairing, took matters into their own hands. On Christmas Day 1990, they brought in materials and machinery, and built their own road. The government reckons it's not up to standard, but when I compare the surface of the new road with that of the old road up to the pass, I can't help wondering what the government is so upset about. Tate's Cairn Tunnel has obscured the old start further down. Alas for the orange groves.

The Maclehose Trail threads its way along this range, avoiding the tops rather than visiting them. The only one it tackles squarely is Beacon Hill, which leaves the others free for the more adventurous, and, of course, for the telecommunications equipment which has proliferated on nearly all the tops around the harbour.

Never mind: Lion Rock is untouched so far. Sunlight on the two crags below the shaggy head has led climbers to christen them Golden Wall (facing south-west) and Brazen Wall (facing south-east). The

above sea level and its foot encroaches on the back gardens of Kowloon Tong. The west ridge of the mountain rises steeply from the pass, and even an expert rock climber would be hard put to it to keep strictly to the crest, going over all the knobs of rock on the skyline. The path takes a less adventurous course among the bushes a few yards to the left of the ridge, bringing you on to the summit after about twenty minutes' climbing from the pass, or an hour and a quarter from Kowloon Tong. Just below the top it is worth scrambling along a rock ledge a little way round on to the precipitous south face of the mountain, where a most impressive view is obtained of the tremendous overhang of rock from which the hill takes its name.

Eastward of Lion Rock are Temple Hill and Tate's Cairn, which are little more than humps on the ridge. Beyond Tate's Cairn the ridge bends sharply to the southward and continues over Middle Hill to the bold pyramid of **Kowloon Peak** (1,971 feet) the highest point on the range. It can easily be reached along the ridge from the north, but a more interesting route is up the steep south face of the mountain. If you follow the Clear Water Bay road to where it forks at the top of the hill behind the Kowloon Dairy, and from there strike straight up the grassy hillside to the left, you will come after two or three hundred feet of scrambling to a faint track slanting across the face of the peak. This bends to the left at first, and then zigzags steeply up beside the splendid crag on the shoulder below the summit. If you fail to find the track, and do not possess nailed shoes and a fairly steady head, it is as well not to attempt this face of Kowloon Peak; a party once got into difficulties here and had to be rescued with a rope.

The whole range from Kowloon Reservoir to Kowloon Peak, five miles or more in length, can be covered in a long day's walk; only the presence of the smoky city, always in sight below you, mars the enjoyment of this expedition. Perhaps on a moonlit night the charm of these hills could be recaptured.

To the north of the range, around the head of Tide Cove, there is some delightful country; Shatin is the best starting point from which to explore this district. From the railway station a bund runs south-eastward to

climb up from Kowloon Pass takes some beating, but be careful. The notice on the fence warns you not to go all the way up, for good reason. Many more people than before visit this peak, and very few of them are as experienced as Graham Heywood. People get killed because they venture too far and then slip or can't get back to safety.

Lo Hsiang-lin researched earlier names for the hills of this ridge, and concluded that Lion Rock was previously known as Tiger-head Hill:

It lies north of Kowloon Chai of Kuan-fu, and is also known as Otter-head Hill. It is full of curious rocks of varying sizes, with precipitous cliffs piercing into the sky. Although difficult of access, it forms the gateway of important routes of communication.

Rather confusingly, Beacon Hill (which Lo Hsiang-lin says is also called Big Fire Hill and Smoke Signal Furnace Hill) used to be called Lion Ridge. Lo writes in *Hong Kong and its External Communications before 1842*:

Lion Ridge is by the side of the Lung-t'ang Village, and extends for over a *li* in length. Here can be seen a rock, standing erect with jagged outlines. Whenever clouds hang upon it, rain follows. During the reign of K'ang-hsi, it marked the limit of removal. The ruin of the signalling furnace is still visible, and helps to give another name to the hill—Beacon Hill.

Lo also mentions Golden Phoenix Hill, Camel Hill, and Sickle-mouth Hill as alternative names, but I'm not clear which of the two hills they would apply to. The 'limit of removal' mentioned in the passage above is a reminder of the Coastal Evacuation from 1662–9, when all the people living on or near the coast were forcibly evicted from their homes by the Manchus in an attempt to deprive pirates and bandits (i.e., Ming dynasty loyalists) of support. The beacon was a lookout post established by the Manchus to keep watch over the area south of the ridge.

Kowloon Peak (Fei Ngo Shan, Flying Goose Hill) is one of my favourites. Taxi from Choi Hung MTR. Stop at the Cha Liu Au road junction (140727). The south face route goes to your left through Mr Mao's gate and up a little path on the right through the trees—on top in an hour for a splendid view. As Graham suggests, use 'sensible caution' about sticking to the path. I once started lower down the road, where there's a group of boulders used for climbing practice. My track petered out, leaving me alternately thrashing through dense grass between rock outcrops and scrabbling frantically for holds on greasy, crumbly rock. Not recommended.

You don't need nailed boots for Kowloon Peak. My girlfriend did this walk wearing ballet shoes. On that day, we were passed by six big guys wearing heavy alpine gear and all roped up. She asked me if we should be dressed like that, and looked dubious when I said no. Later we stopped to watch them on Suicide Wall, the big slab higher up. One began abseiling down the crag without anyone on the top end of his rope. He slipped and slid 15 feet down the crag with only his nose in contact. Their T-shirts carried

a footbridge over the little estuary which opens into Tide Cove. At low tide a wide expanse of mangrove swamps and mud-flats is exposed, and half the local population goes out to dig for shellfish. A walk of a couple of miles around the shore beyond the footbridge will bring you to a bay overlooked by Buffalo Hill. You can make a good round by climbing up to **Heather Pass** (1,227 feet), which is the gap to the south of Buffalo Hill, leading over to Port Shelter. It is a steep climb up through the woods to the pass, but you are rewarded by the glorious view over Port Shelter which suddenly confronts you as you reach the crest. There is always a thrill of expectation when you are nearing a pass and wondering what you will see on the far side, and the view from this pass is one of the best I know in the New Territories. From Heather Pass it is an easy walk along the high ground to the south, and so home across the Kowloon range. Or you may make a longer expedition by descending to Hebe Haven down a charming valley to the eastward of the pass. Here you will reach the Sai Kung road. Failing a lift by car or truck, you will have to walk home over Customs Pass, another ascent of about 800 feet; this is rather a grind at the end of a day's walking, but much of the way is cool and shady, and passes through charming country. The stones of the old paved path have been worn smooth by the tread of thousands of feet. Paths such as as these are still the only means of communication between most of the villages in the New Territories, as they were, I suppose, in England before the days of wheeled traffic; travel must then have been a quiet and leisurely affair.

Instead of climbing to Heather Pass from Tide Cove, you can leave Buffalo Hill on your right and walk up a gently sloping valley to **Turret Pass** (845 feet). Ma On Shan looks its best from here, framed in the trees which shade the pass. On the north side of the pass you come down to a little village named Mui Tsz Lam, standing in a deep and narrow valley. The quickest way home from here is to turn left-handed down the valley to Tai Shui Hang, at the foot of Ma On Shan, and chance getting a sampan there to take you across Tide Cove to the Shatin road.

If you are feeling energetic and have plenty of time to spare, it is a fine walk to turn right-handed at

the name of a big Himalayan peak in China, so we hoped they were still practising.

Paths also go up Kowloon Peak from the roads to east and west, that from the east being much the easiest to find and follow. In the Pak Fa Lam cemetery just below the start of that path is a locally venerated landmark, the grave of Dr. Sun Yat-sen's mother.

On the left of the path northwards along the ridge from Kowloon Peak, about 200 yards after you pass Middle Hill, there's a strange shaped rock that makes a fine perch for a refreshment stop. From the road below it looks like a giant's gaunt face. Down to your left, you can glimpse a little tea house amongst the trees above the road.

Surely the best part of the walk along the ridge above Kowloon is the tremendous view of the city below. Part of the outing's charm is the ever-present contrast between grey and green, between the bustle of the city and the quiet of the country, the neon city glare and the soft moonlight.

How I wish I had the chance, as Graham did, to see the Sha Tin citizens digging for shellfish at low tide. There wouldn't be enough shellfish to go round, even if they survived in the foul waters of Shing Mun River Channel, as the murky remnant of Tide Cove has been renamed. This is Hong Kong's only straight stretch of calm water, so the rowing club holds weekend practice sessions here.

I bought a pack of postcards from To Fung Shan one day and found that it included a view of Tide Cove from Amah Rock before

the new town was built—quite a contrast. Rice from this valley used to be sent to the Emperor, and was so famous that competitors used to fraudulently claim that theirs was 'Sha Tin rice'. Nineteen villages marked on pre-war maps have been left in Sha Tin, unlike Tsuen Wan where only one remains. Walking round the old coastline you'll find that nearly all the old houses have been replaced, although you can still see one row of traditional village houses at Pai Tau, next to the access ramp to Shatin KCR station. Yuen Chau Kok, and two other significant *fung shui* hills, have survived.

Looking at the map, it's hard to distinguish which way Graham would have gone up to Heather Pass. Possibly there used to be a way over the pass between the villages of Lo Shue Tin and Tai No. Going down to Hebe Haven involves a bit of a detour, but it's a pleasant walk down the valley. There's an attractive waterfall hidden in the trees next to the path, visible from One Rise More.

The old road over Customs Pass goes up the Ho Chung Valley. As you might expect, not many people use it nowadays, and you will have it all to yourself as you walk upstream. (There's a stretch in the middle, between 153744 and 152742, where it's been hijacked and fenced off by a squatter.) Locals knew the lower part of this stream as the 'Black River' for many years because of a dyeing works that discharged untreated waste; it's now closed, and the blackened stones in the river bed have regained some of their natural hues.

Mui Tsz Lam, and climb the valley to **Delta Pass** at its head. This pass crosses the range between Buffalo Hill and Ma On Shan, and leads over to Sai Kung, the fishing harbour on Port Shelter, now connected with Kowloon by road.

I have still to mention the range of hills overlooking Tide Cove on the west. The back-bone of this range can be reached from Shatin in about an hour by turning left off the main Tai Po road just short of the level crossing, and following a lane up the hill. The lane leads to a Buddhist-Christian institute known as Tao Fong Shan, a dignified and beautiful group of buildings in the Chinese style finely situated on a spur of the hill. The lane continues to climb beyond Tao Fong Shan; follow it as far as a small bungalow, then take a path to the right. Keeping mainly to the crest of the spur, the skyline can be reached with little difficulty.

Along the ridge to the left is the upstanding peak of **Needle Hill** (1,741 feet), overlooking Shing Mun reservoir; this point can also be climbed in an hour from the Shing Mun dam. To the right the ridge rises gradually to the broad and rather undistinguished summit of **Grassy Hill** (2,144 feet). Although this is the third highest peak in the New Territories, it is seldom visited by walkers.

Turret Pass gives a fine view of Ma On Shan, and it must look even better from Turret Hill. You might also try Shek Nga Shan which comes down from Buffalo Hill, providing an interesting walk over a series of ridge bumps, and ending near Fa Sam Hang after a bit of a thrash through scrub.

The valley up to Delta Pass from Mui Tsz Lam is a delight. Delta Pass (163780) is a victim of mapmakers' amnesia, being indicated only by a 'Picnic site (Barbecue prohibited)' symbol near the old village school, now disused and demolished. On the Sai Kung side, the Tin Hau temple and the name of Pak Kung village (North Harbour), may indicate that the sea once came all the way inland.

There are many paths up to the range between Needle Hill and Grassy Hill. To be honest, neither of these hills is visited just for the pleasure of it, but both get thousands of visitors every year because they're on the Maclehose Trail. Grassy Hill is especially frustrating—it's one of those hills where just as you think you're getting to the top, the road goes round a bend and you see that the top is there in front of you; then, just as you reach it, there's another bend and another top . . . .

Since Graham wrote, we have been given the Tai Po Kau Nature Reserve, several square miles of mature woodland, home to birds, butterflies, and animals of all kinds. You can get a booklet to accompany the Nature Trail and four colour-coded forest walks. One of the *Twelve Hong Kong Walks* takes you around the Reserve in December.

South of Kowloon Peak, the line of hills to Devil's Peak makes a nice afternoon stroll. Miss the one with the quarries, Tai Sheung Tok, and begin at Black Hill. Devil's Peak was the site of a wartime heavy gun battery, placed to deter enemy ships that never came. In *Hong Kong Eclipse* (Oxford University Press, 1978) by G. B. Endacott, there's a photo of the Japanese commander looking over here from the island during the final phase of the 1941 attack. Lo says that Devil's Peak used to be called Chi-p'o Shan, Old Hen Hill. He also introduces the Ming loyalist turned pirate who entrenched himself here after a resounding victory over Manchu troops in 1679:

Because of his devilish cunning and his love of fighting, the hill where Cheng Lien-ch'ang encamped came to be called Devil's Peak. He also built on the shore of Li-yu men a temple dedicated to the Goddess of Heaven. At the back of this temple is a secret cave in Devil's Hill, probably the hiding place for his treasures.

CHAPTER V.

MA ON SHAN.

Of all the Hong Kong hills Ma On Shan is my favourite; its steep wooded slopes falling straight to the sea, and the graceful curve of the skyline between its two peaks, make it the most beautiful of our mountains. It is a fine climb by any route, and on a clear day the view from the summit is unsurpassed; to the west Tai Mo Shan shows its full height; to the north-east, seeming almost beneath one's feet so steep is the slope, lies Tolo Channel, and beyond it are blue hills and blue water along miles of coast to Bias Bay in the distance.

The Hunchback Ridge. The south and west sides of Ma On Shan can most easily be reached by taking a sampan from Lok Lo Ha, about a mile and a half beyond Shatin on the Tai Po road. The voyage across Tide Cove takes twenty minutes or so, and is a pleasant way of beginning and ending a day's scrambling. Some bargaining will be necessary to secure a sampan at a reasonable price; two dollars used to be the fare for the return trip for a small party; ten will now be demanded. The sampan lands you at Tai Shui Hang, the village on the far shore, and there it will wait for your return. The path goes through the village and up on to the hill to the left of the last house; it winds along the side of a valley some distance above the stream until it joins the Iron Mine road near Ma On Shan village. The road is followed for a few hundred yards westward to the foot of the Hunchback Ridge—the left-hand ridge in the sketch; a faint track can be discovered making for the rocks of the first hunchback. This is a delectable place for the lunch halt, where the climber can recline on sun-warmed rocks, while dangling his feet over the edge of the cliff a hundred feet or so above the tree-tops.

For the remainder of the way the path follows the ridge—a most airy and exhilarating climb. The second hunchback is steep and requires a moderately steady head; nailed shoes will give a sense of security which is lacking in the handholds of straggling grass. There are some fine buttresses of rock on the seaward side of the ridge, and it is possible to reach this point

52

Commentary—Chapter 5

YES, it's beautiful. No need to say more.

Your approach to the Hunchback Ridge will be different from Graham's. No sampans from Lok Lo Ha to Tai Shui Hang any more; there is now a bridge across the mouth of the inlet. Lok Lo Ha is a mile from the sea. The whole of the northern end of the Ma On Shan peninsula is a construction site—roads and high-rise blocks are altering the coastline out of recognition. Every time I go, there's a new housing estate going up.

If you really want to take a sampan, there is a service from Ma Liu Shui (follow the signs from University KCR station) to Wu Kai Sha, north of the Hunchbacks, but it's a terribly dreary trudge from there to the proper start of the walk. If you thought of following Graham by boat, forget it and catch the 85K bus from Sha Tin KCR. Bargaining for the fare will not be necessary or permitted. Spare a glance at the Sha Tin Fishermen's New Village, which once gave its inhabitants a new home by the sea when Sha Tin became landlocked, but which has in its turn been left stranded behind even newer reclamation. Get off the bus at Chevalier Garden (Tai Shui Hang), from where Graham made his way over the foothills.

I haven't been able to find any of the paths which according to the map start from near Tai Shui Hang, so I suggest you follow the waterworks road from 139808 up to the little dam at 147806, cross over the stream, and climb the flight of steps up the far side. The way is fairly obvious, though a little overgrown, and brings you out by a cluster of farms in a hollow of the hills opposite Ma On Shan Tsuen. Cross the stream again, and turn left when you join the road. Walk through the lower village and back towards the coast until you reach the leisure area/barbecue site at the foot of the ridge. I've found two ways up the Hunchbacks from here, although I'm still looking for a better one, because neither is clear or obvious.

The first route starts on the other, northeast, side of the leisure area. Walk up through the trees (there's no path) until you get to the large water catchment marking the upper edge of the newest trees. Find the highest point on the catchment, and follow a path from there which heads for the rocks on the skyline, the first hunchback. After a few yards, the path trends left as it follows an erosion bank. Where the erosion bank turns right, the path goes straight up the hillside from the corner, and eventually reaches the ridge just below the first hunchback (to the west of it, to its left, as you look at it from below).

The second route starts from the road to the southeast of the leisure area. At the end of the road is a house with many dogs. The dogs will bark madly, and you may wish to wait until someone has come out to restrain them before you go any further. To the left of the house is a gully. Go up the gully, find the little path round the back of the fence, and a few yards after the little path has become a bigger path, go left up a gully and climb up the hillside.

direct from the coast up one of the gullies between the cliffs, but it is difficult going. This part of the mountain is famed for its rhododendrons; in March and April there is a beautiful show of the common brick-red species, *Rhododendron indicum,* while here and there are bushes of *R. farrerae,* a mountain species which flowers before it comes into leaf. Three rare and lovely species may be found amongst the thickets—*R. fordii,* an evergreen with pink flowers, *R. westlandii,* which grows to the size of a tree, and has very large pale pink flowers, and *R. ovatum,* whose pure white flowers are the most beautiful of all.

The third and highest hunchback (2,226 feet) is reached in about 2½ hours from Tai Shui Hang. A narrow curving ridge still separates you from the highest point of Ma On Shan. It is from this ridge that the mountain takes its name, which means "Horse Saddle Peak." A further 20 minutes walking will take you to the summit (2,261 feet); I must have visited it twenty times; it never fails to delight me, for a mountain, like an old friend, grows in one's affections every time one meets it.

The short cut directly down the south-west face towards Ma On Shan village looks simple, but is not to be recommended; I have vivid recollections of a nightmare struggle to reach the stream through thick scrub, where spiders of incredible size would appear suddenly a few inches in front of my face. A better way is to continue along the ridge and so down to the Iron Mine by the route described in the next paragraph.

The South Ridge. An easy way up the mountain starts from the unsightly Iron Mine about half a mile south-east of Ma On Shan village, which can be reached from Tai Shui Hang by the path already described. When you strike the road, follow it to the right as far as the mine; beyond this point a path crosses a shoulder of the hill into a narrow valley which descends from the high ground immediately to the south of the summit (see sketch). The path crosses a stream and zig-zags up a grassy spur on the far side, eventually reaching a high pass on the ridge between Ma On Shan and Pyramid Hill. The ridge is followed to the top, passing close to the fine crag which falls sheer from the summit on its eastern side. Time, 2½ hours from Tai Shui

COMMENTARY

Country Parks and the Maclehose Trail

Few tourists realise that nearly 50 per cent of Hong Kong is occupied by country parks. It's not a publicised attraction, which I think is a pity. True, many of Hong Kong's visitors do go to Lantau and the New Territories, expecting and getting a pleasant day off from shopping.

Hong Kong's residents are often equally uninformed; a survey of my office colleagues reveals that some have never been beyond Lion Rock. However, this is changing, and country parks received 9.3 million visitors in 1990, well up from 2.3 million in 1976. There are picnic sites, barbecue pits, visitor centres, litter bins, and signposts to cater for all sorts of visitors—those who just drive out and cook lunch as well as those who spend all day hiking.

Sir Murray Maclehose, governor from 1971 to 1982, was a keen lover of the outdoors, and an enthusiastic supporter of any attempts to get people out there. He played a major role in setting up the country parks, the establishment of which is described by Stella Thrower in her excellent introduction to the countryside, Hong Kong Country Parks *(Government Information Services, 1984).*

In honour of Maclehose's efforts, Hong Kong's first long-distance footpath was named after him. The Maclehose Trail rather inelegantly traces its way through 100 kms (62 miles) of the New Territories. The route is a bit artificial, and includes at both ends some stunningly boring sections which must have been added on merely to get to the magic '100'. The sections in the middle are challenging and pass through some of Hong Kong's best scenery.

The Maclehose Trail exhibits the usual problems associated with long-distance footpaths: a tendency for walkers to stick rigidly to the designated path, the abandonment of other footpaths, excessive erosion, and litter.

Hang. My memories of this route are chiefly of rollicking descents, when we scrambled down the steep summit ridge, and then threw caution to the winds in a wild rush down the dusty zig-zags to the little stream; here we could drink our fill, and bathe and get dry again in the evening sunshine.

The East Face from Sai Kung. Seen from Port Shelter, the bold eastern face of Ma On Shan looks forbiddingly steep, yet there is an easy path up the mountain from this side, which should become popular now that Sai Kung is accessible by road. Rather less than a mile north of Sai Kung a long wooded spur comes down to the coast, and a paved path leads up its southern flank to the village of Wong Chuk Yeung, about 700 feet above sea level. I reached this village one evening with about two hours of daylight to spare; the clouds were so low that the blue smoke from the cottages was rising into the grey blanket of mist which lay close above the roofs. I asked a villager the way up the mountain; he evidently thought that this mad Westerner should be discouraged from wandering on the hills so late in the evening in so thick a fog, and told me so that there was no way. Not wishing to worry the kind man, I retraced my steps until out of sight, and then scrambled through the bushes to an obvious path on the hillside behind the village. This took me on to a spur and along a hummocky ridge towards the face of the mountain, with fine glimpses through the mist of the cliffs below the summit away to the right. The path turned to the left where the ridge joins the face, and finally reached the crest of the south ridge about 500 yards from the summit. This climb takes about 2 hours from Sai Kung.

So much for the easy ways up Ma On Shan, which can be climbed all (or very nearly all) the way with the hands in the pockets.

The North-East Face. This splendid mountain wall is thickly forested and difficult of access, but the botanist or scrambler will find it well worth a visit. This side of the mountain may be reached by a walk of some five miles from Sai Kung over to Three Fathom Cove, and thence along the coast, or by taking a sampan from Lok Lo Ha to the Iron Mine jetty and approaching from the opposite direction by a two-mile

You should be following a faint track through the scrub heading, again, for the rocks of the first hunchback. This track reaches the ridge at the col just above the first hunchback (to the east, or right).

Here I confess I'm surprised by Graham. Is he really proposing to have lunch so early? Even though it's a steep pull up to the ridge and I would heartily approve of pausing here for a breather and a piece of chocolate, I'd have thought we might get a bit higher before we stop for lunch. The ridge will require care and concentration. And extra care if it's been raining. You don't need nailed shoes—a pair of trainers or shoes with a grip will suffice.

Graham writes: 'It is possible to reach this point direct from the coast up one of the gullies between the cliffs'. Here I confess I'm amazed by Graham. Go and take a look over the edge. Do you fancy it? The paths shown on the map are, as far as I can see, totally fictitious. Not being an expert in rhododendrons, I can't tell you which particular species have made ascent on this side impossible, but the March walk in *Twelve Hong Kong Walks* has all the details. Higher up this ridge one day, we came across a family picking fruits from the trees. They gave us one or two, which we found tasty but couldn't identify.

The Chinese name of the Hunchbacks is Niu Ya Shan, or Ox Mortgage Hill; nobody has been able to explain to me why the ox was mortgaged. The first hunchback has its own alternative name—Tiu Shau Ngam, or Hanging Hand Crag.

You'll be wise if you take Graham's advice about the short-cut. Don't be tempted by short-cuts in Hong Kong; they usually result in cuts to the hands, arms, legs, and face. It sounds as if this area was overgrown in Graham's day, but it's even worse now. And the spiders haven't got any smaller either.

The path up the South Ridge is still visible, but the main route from the Iron Mine side of the hill now goes up to the col at 165794, where there is a junction with the Maclehose Trail. You reach the ridge via a set of zigzags immediately north of Pyramid Hill after contouring around its northwest flank.

After a night at Chinese New Year camping out below Pyramid Hill (in Chinese, Ngong Ping Hill or Big Money Hill), I scrambled to the top for breakfast. The view is magnificent to east, south, and west, the effect of the height heightened by the steepness of the slope. As you watch the town coming to life far below, you feel smugly virtuous at having got so much done so early in the day.

As Graham predicted, the most popular modern approach to Ma On Shan is via the Maclehose Trail up the East Face from Sai Kung. However, the Trail doesn't go to the summit, so neither do most of the walkers. It turns left when it reaches the ridge, and perhaps the walkers are deterred by the impressive crag which towers over their approach. Near the start of this route is the village of Long Keng, where there is said to be Hong Kong's oldest and largest sacred banyan tree.

You can catch an air-conditioned

walk around the base of the Hunchbacks. There is a choice of two routes up the north-east face, one leading to the top of Ma On Shan and the other to the top of the Hunchbacks, both of which are real mountain climbs; the difficulties however, are due as much to the thickness of the scrub as to the steepness of the ground.

The first of these routes starts from the village of Tai Tung; the valley is followed for a little way beyond the village to the foot of a narrow spur, which runs up to the great amphitheatre of cliffs below the summit ridge. Our party climbed the rough track up the crest of the spur until we reached the foot of the cliffs. Here further ascent seemed to be cut off, but a ledge was found, leading away to the left through thick bushes to a rocky shoulder. We scrambled up this, taking comfort from the thought that had we slipped on the wet and greasy rocks the bushes would have prevented us from rolling far. It was an exciting bit of climbing, but it was soon over, to the disappointment of the rock-climber of the party and the relief of the others. Above was a steep slope of grass, and before long we emerged, breathless and triumphant, on the summit of Ma On Shan.

It was on this occasion that we had the good fortune to see the Brocken Spectre, a very beautiful optical effect which sometimes appears when one looks down on sunlit mists from above. All the lower hills to the east were covered with a thick blanket of cloud, whose edges were swirling up the slopes below the summit. As we came down the ridge the sun threw our shadows on to the mists, and each of us saw rings of rainbow light surrounding the shadow of his head.

The summit of the Hunchbacks can also be reached from the north-east by a spur which rises from sea-level at Nai Chung village, and runs parallel to the one just described. Another steep and exhilarating climb, but decidedly an energetic one.

A quick way off the Hunchbacks is to take the north-west ridge, which plunges straight down from the highest point almost to sea-level. A narrow track follows the edge of the ridge, like a long rabbit-hole through the bushes. When it reaches a grassy shoulder about 1,000 feet above the sea, the track bears right

bus now from Sha Tin towards Sai Kung and disembark wherever you feel it would be most convenient for the north-east face. Although the map asserts there are several paths up this side of Ma On Shan, I never took it seriously enough to actually get off a bus until the beginning of 1992, when over a drizzly Chinese New Year, I went to check the routes out. The map shows tracks from Tai Tung, Ma Kwu Lam, and Nai Chung. There's no sign of the last one—the spur is completely overgrown and impassable. The second wanders across an overgrown wilderness of abandoned paddy fields overlooked by graves, and then disappears.

The first might go, but here I confess I'm astounded by Graham. He was the rock climber of the party which tackled this face direct from Tai Tung. In early 1992 the spur just beyond the village is bare from a recent fire, but in view of Graham's comments, it will definitely have to wait for a fine day and company. If I'm going to go gallivanting on wet and greasy rocks at a 70 degree angle, I want a witness. Even if you don't venture up the spur to try the climb, the walk up the valley to Tai Tung Wo Liu is nice. It takes you deep into the hills, and there is a magnificent view of cloud-shrouded crags. If you wondered about Graham's ability, go and look at these climbs, but don't go up alone.

The western side of Ma On Shan achieved brief notoriety in 1988, when tigers were seen one Sunday morning by two construction workers. In the ensuing search, the police shot and killed two stray dogs, whereupon the RSPCA demanded to know why they had not been using tranquilliser guns, since tigers are a protected species. The day after this fracas, the vet of the Jockey Club at Sha Tin wondered whether the 'tigers' could have been his two Irish wolfhounds, Duncan and Jenny, whom he had taken for a walk. The construction workers, gingerly inspecting the dogs, finally conceded that they might have panicked and jumped to the wrong conclusion, although they pointed out that the wolfhounds bore a striking resemblance to tigers. The search was called off and no more was said.

The Iron Mine operated between 1949 and 1976. Many refugees from northern China worked here, part of a labour force of up to 5,000 organised in three shifts, doing a day's work for thirty cents and two meals. But wages were only paid after three months, so most of the time the workers got just a handful of rice each day. The mine closed six years before the lease expired, with only one-third of the reserves extracted. The market for their iron had been Japanese ship-building yards producing supertankers, but the oil price rises of the 1970s slashed demand for supertankers and the Japanese yards were forced to cut back. Two hundred retired workers still live around the village, unwilling to move from familiar surroundings.

I once camped out above the Iron Mine during Chinese New Year on my way from Kowloon Peak to Sharp Peak. I'd rejected the Ngong Ping campsite as being too noisy,

and descends towards White Head. If your sampan is waiting for you at the jetty, you will be tempted to take a short cut to the left, across the lower slopes of the mountain. But the hillside is thickly forested and almost impassable, and the longer way round will prove the quicker way home.

Kowloon Peak to Ma On Shan. There is a charm in a long walk on a high ridge; the uphill grind is finished early, and all day long you are walking in the cool air of the hilltops, with wide views on either side. And when at last you reach the final point of the ridge and look back on the long rank of peaks and passes which you have crossed, you feel that the day has indeed been well spent. Perhaps the finest walk in the Colony is from Kowloon Peak to Ma On Shan, along the watershed which divides Port Shelter on the east from Tide Cove and Hong Kong Harbour on the west. The ridge is never less than 1,000 feet above sea level; from end of end it is five miles as the crow flies, and the whole walk, returning by Sai Kung and over Customs Pass, is about 16 miles in length. A peak-bagger, who delights in climbing as many summits as possible in the day, will of course walk over every point on the ridge; this would involve over 5,000 feet of ascent—rather too enormous an expedition for an ordinary walker. We started at 9.30 a.m., and took an easier way, missing Kowloon Peak itself, and reaching the ridge by the Jat Incline. This was then a path, but is now a road; it starts from the Clear Water Bay road a short distance above the Kowloon Dairy, and climbs for 1,700 feet at an easy gradient across the flank of Kowloon Peak, joining the Shatin Pass road near the crest of the ridge. We reached the ridge to the south-east of Tate's Cairn in 1¾ hours from the bus stop at Kai Tak.

A few steps down on the far side put us out of sight of the town, and we might have been a hundred miles from civilization. This is certainly the place for a halt, to gaze on the lovely view over Port Shelter; but not a long one, for Ma On Shan, at the end of the range beyond Buffalo Hill, is still far away. The next obstacle was the little hill obscurely named One Rise More; we decided that we could do with one rise less, and refused to clamber to the top of the hillock with the odd name. It was avoided by skirting it to the west along a path which passes just above Mau Tso

and was looking for a quiet flat spot somewhere among the rocks below the path. Finding that paths provided the only flat spots, I camped on the most minor path I could find. Shouldn't be disturbed, I thought, as I cooked up some spaghetti 'maonshannaise' and watched the fireworks going off over Victoria Harbour seven miles away. In the middle of the night I was woken up by a discussion. Five or six men were waving torches about and wondering why there was a tent in the middle of the path. I was too sleepy to be frightened and, more intrigued than scared, I listened as they concluded that it had to be an illusion, skirted round above the path, and went on their way.

Two years ago, my cousin persuaded me to usher in my 40th birthday with an overnight bivouac on Ma On Shan. We celebrated dawn with rum and Coke and birthday cake next to the summit trig point. There's something very satisfying but hard to explain about eating on hilltops. The location seems to give a new perspective to everyday activity.

Kowloon Peak to Ma On Shan is a wonderful walk. The Maclehose Trail has eliminated route-finding problems between Buffalo Hill and Delta Pass. That apart, the surroundings are so unchanged and the directions are so clear, it's as if Graham were walking next to you, whispering in your ear. The only people you meet on this walk will be other walkers. The village of Ngong Ping was abandoned years ago, leaving barely a stone to mark its place. A campsite was

established on the old paddy fields for Maclehose Trailwalkers. The descendants of Graham's cows browse around the tents, where campers enliven the day with radios and happy conversation.

Sai Kung—now there's a changed place. Graham might even have preferred 'Ye Olde Ship Inne' to the uncontrolled sprawl that has steadily smothered the western shores of Port Shelter. And better access has brought the modern world across Customs Pass and into this rural enclave. The villagers have benefited, and so have the Cathay Pacific airline staff and all the others who can now live here with convenient access to the city. And so have the sailors who can keep their boats secure in Hebe Haven and enjoy weekends exploring the islands and inlets of the rugged coast to the east.

There is an occasional temptation that grips those who seek out solitude and wild places. Every so often, particularly when faced with a reminder of what we conceive the world was like before it was 'spoilt', we have a desire to turn the clock back. Let's pause, here above Sai Kung, and examine this temptation.

Those who most regret the passing of old ways of life are city-dwellers: people with enough money to have leisure, and comfortable houses to return to and relax in after a sweaty day out in the country. Looking at the romantic picture of the rustic idyll from the outside, they sometimes don't realise what a hard life it used to be and still can be. However, the romantic picture has never been accurate for those living

Ngam village, and so down to Heather Pass. A few yards below this pass to the east is a spring which is always running except in the driest of seasons; here we did justice to a magnificent thirst.

A paved path runs eastward from Heather Pass across the slopes of Buffalo Hill to Buffalo Pass. As far as I know, there is no path to the top of **Buffalo Hill** (1,987 feet), but this glorious viewpoint can be reached fairly easily by a steep scramble of 400 feet up from the pass of the same name. After this digression we returned to the pass and continued along the ridge; the route was a little vague, for the good path had descended into the valley on our left, and we had to trust to cow tracks. In clear weather there is no difficulty in following the watershed down to Delta Pass; unfortunately, however, we were by this time shrouded in thick mist. We passed some cows placidly browsing in the fog, and continued to plod ahead, wishing we had a compass. It soon became obvious to the rearguard that the leader, although he obstinately went on marching, had lost the way. In a little while some more cows loomed up in the mist; they looked strangely familiar, and closer examination proved without any doubt that they were the very cows which we had passed a quarter of an hour previously. After this chastening experience we pulled ourselves together, and found our way to Delta Pass without further mishap. Here we halted for half an hour for lunch.

On the far side of the pass is a short steep rise to Ngong Ping. This remote little village has a charm of its own; it stands on a high plateau, hidden from the rest of the world; a grove shades it in summer, and shelters it from the east wind in winter; in front are a few paddy fields, and beyond them are only the mountain tops and the wide sky.

The path crosses the paddy fields, goes over a pass west of Pyramid Hill, and descends to Ma On Shan village; we left it a few yards below the pass on the far side and took an easy short cut across the hillside in the direction of the summit of Ma On Shan, until we struck the path up from the Iron Mine. The route from here to the summit has already been described. We reached the top in thick cloud at 2.45 p.m., halted long enough to eat an orange, and turned back to

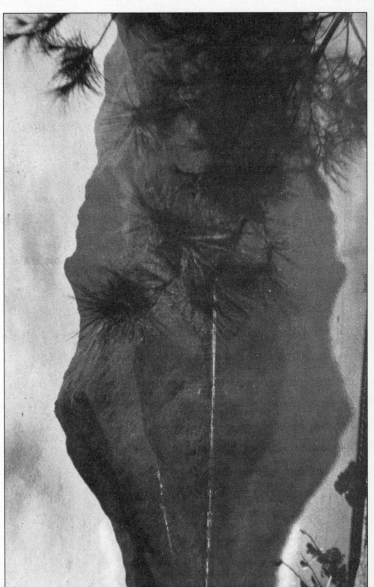

Photo. A. Payne

Ma On Shan

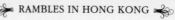

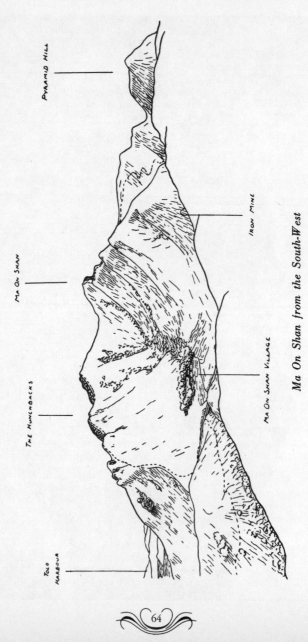

PYRAMID HILL

IRON MINE

MA ON SHAN

MA ON SHAN VILLAGE

THE HUNCHBACKS

TOLO HARBOUR

Ma On Shan from the South-West

within it. As if to spite those who want to preserve the past, country-dwellers almost everywhere eagerly accept any changes that bring them prosperity and opportunity.

Let's find, if we can, a way to allow others to benefit while still being able to enjoy ourselves. There is a way. Faced with that desire to turn the clock back, content yourself with your imagination, which you are allowed to make as rustic as you like.

Close your eyes, and picture to yourself the scene in pre-war days, when the tarmac stopped at Customs Pass, and Sai Kung was the start of the back of beyond, and boats were the main form of transport to all points east. Indulge in this image, and wonder all you like about what's gone. But then open your eyes and your lungs, take a deep breath of fresh air, and just be grateful that this marvellous walk is still available to blow away the cobwebs from the corners of your busy modern life.

Trailwalker

Every year since 1981, normally sensible men and women have run, walked, stumbled, crawled, and bled their way along the Maclehose Trail, punishing themselves in aid of others. Trailwalker is a charity outing; participants travel in teams of four, with forty-eight hours to complete the 100 kilometres. It was started by the army, then taken up by a few intrepid civilians in 1986, and is now open to all comers. In 1990, more than 400 teams joined in, raising $6 million; in 1991, some 500 teams raised $7 million.

What's the point? Besides raising money for a deserving cause, it's a personal challenge. I suppose you'd get as many different answers as there are people doing the event. Some run as fast as they can; others walk steadily, taking the full 48 hours to finish.

The Queen's Gurkha Signals regimental team that came first in 1990 set a record of 13 hours and 21 minutes, stopping on the way for only 25 minutes. They did it for the honour of their unit, and were given plenty of time off to prepare for the run. According to the South China Morning Post *of 22 September, in1991, 16 Gurkha wives signed up: '"We want to raise money for the underprivileged in Nepal and Hong Kong," said Mrs Padura Lama, 28. She said the women have a diet to follow. "One piece of toast for breakfast," she said."Tuna, toast and tea for lunch and a slice of meat and salad in the evening."'*

In 1989, a blind man and his team-mate were the stars:

The South China Morning Post *reported on October 30, 'Twenty-year-old Lau Chung-wai was undoubtedly the toast of Trailwalker '89 yesterday ... Without any pre-training along the treacherous, rock-strewn Maclehose Trail, he became the first blind person to enter—and finish ...Mr Lau was led all the way by Mr Chan Sing-chung, who suffers from cerebral palsy. They finished the race in 46 hours and 40 minutes ... He said enjoyment was the main objective: "It's not that difficult if you enjoy yourself."'*

descend to Sai Kung. It was pleasant to come down out of the cloud on to lower ground; the greens and browns of the hillsides were good to look on, for colours never seem so rich as when the eyes have been attuned for hours to a grey monotone of mist.

The fishing fleet was anchored in the little harbour of Sai Kung, and from the junks came a cheerful clack of voices like the contented sounds from a rookery in the evening. If Sai Kung were transplanted to the south coast of England, it would become a "beauty spot"; artists would inhabit the cottages; "Ye Olde Ship Inne" would inevitably make its appearance, with its ruinous prices and sham antiques, and at its doors charabancs would unload their hordes at week-ends. But away with such horrid thoughts; Sai Kung was still cut off from civilization by six miles of footpath, and though we could not get beer to revive us for the long trudge home, at least we could get delicious oranges for next to nothing.

Thus refreshed, we strolled home in the dusk over Customs Pass, and at 7 p.m. reached the car waiting at the bottom of the hill.

Fisherman

Photo. C. H. Kuhne

CHAPTER VI.

EASTWARD TO MIRS BAY.

The eastern shores of the New Territories, around Port Shelter and Mirs Bay, must appeal to anyone who loves wild places. Here sea and land meet in a tangle of headlands, inlets and islands; Crescent Island, Crooked Harbour, Rocky Harbour—the names bring to mind pictures of rugged coasts washed by seas whose waters are so clear that you can see the colours of the coral fathoms deep. Here and there is a fishing village in a sheltered bay, the houses crowding close together for company in the wilderness. Or you may come upon a little fleet of sampans anchored off a sandy beach, their crews ashore drawing water from a mountain stream, or mending their nets in readiness for the night's fishing. Apart from these you may go for miles without seeing anything of man's handiwork, for the hillsides fall steeply to the sea and there is little room for cultivation.

This remote country is divided into three long irregular peninsulas by the sea inlets of Junk Bay, Port Shelter, Tolo Channel and Starling Inlet. Much of the district is almost inaccessible except by boat, and few of us are lucky enough to cruise so far afield. The southernmost of the three peninsulas, however, was opened up by the construction of the Clear Water Bay road, and recently the central peninsula has become slightly less inaccessible with the opening of a road to Sai Kung. This chapter deals with the two southerly peninsulas, for the remaining one contains the Pat Sin range and the Bride's Pool, and deserves a chapter to itself.

High Junk Peak and Clear Water Bay. The new road to Clear Water Bay is a perpetual delight; familiarity can never spoil the rapturous moment when you top the rise over the shoulder of Razor Hill, and see again the glorious panorama of Ma On Shan standing proudly above the wooded foothills around Sai Kung. And as you go down the road beyond, each corner brings into view another lovely stretch of hills and sea; emerald and turquoise are but a poor simile for the vivid colours that will feast your eyes on a sunny day. One or two of my favourite spots in the Colony

Commentary—Chapter 6

How have Graham's wild places fared? Mixed results where sea and land meet, but much worse underwater. There's been a lot of development on the Port Shelter coast, and the sea has been badly polluted. It's a crying shame that we can't take better care of our ocean—the coral is nearly gone, scuba divers grumble that visibility is down to a few feet, and 'red tides' signal that the sea is poisonous. At least the hills are surviving.

The road to Sai Kung was built by the Japanese between the first and second editions of Graham's book. It has since been extended to Hoi Ha on the northern coast of the Sai Kung peninsula, but remains restricted and has brought little except a bus every hour or so, and better access for village smugglers. The eastern coast remains inaccessible to wheels, and is little changed. The southern coastline has been transformed by the creation of High Island Reservoir, which has ingeniously made a former island (High Island) into a part of the mainland, and at the same time made a former mainland hill (Shui Keng Teng) into an island. Service roads give access on either side of the reservoir.

Graham would find today's Clear Water Bay peninsula very different from the one he knew. Big groups of hikers and campers reassure themselves with loud radios, and modern man seems less than ever contented with silence. The sampan fleets have mostly gone, but the bays are not completely deserted; their anchorages are filled on weekends with pleasure boats. At the southern end of the peninsula, golfers play above the Tin Hau temple and lose their balls to the sea with overambitious drives.

High Junk Peak and Clear Water Bay: What I like about the road to Clear Water Bay is the stretch which goes around in a big circle below Kowloon Peak. The loop wasn't there in Graham's time—it's a modern addition to allow double-decker buses and heavy trucks to get up the hill.

If you sit on the front seat on the upper deck of the bus as it climbs the hill from Choi Hung, you may by craning your neck enjoy the view of the dramatic rock-studded hillside leading up to Suicide Crag. Kowloon Peak so often wears a wild wisp of cloud in the mode of a tam o'shanter, which imparts an air of Scottish grandeur to its slopes. As the bus goes further up the road, it gets more difficult to see the hillside, and finally impossible. Then you suddenly realise that you're going away from the hill, and as the bus traverses the far side of the loop you can have a leisurely second look, much grander than the first.

Just by the prison, there are routes up Razor Hill (in Chinese, Partridge Hill) and Hebe Hill (Piercing Wind Hill), on either side of the main road. For not too much effort, both hills give nice views of the Kowloon range to the west, the Ma On Shan range to the north, and Port Shelter to the east. The paths are overgrown and none too clear, so you might have to explore a bit. I had an inconclusive discussion once about why criminals are kept in such scenic places, while law-lie close to the road, but these I am going to keep selfishly to myself in the hopes that no one else will discover them.

Beyond Razor Hill the road passes along the narrow neck of the most southerly of the three peninsulas. At the foot of the hill to the right is Hang Hau, the fishing village at the head of Junk Bay. The junks in the little harbour anchor two by two—a nice sociable habit.

Although a large area of good country has been opened up by this road, I sometimes sigh for the old days when all this district was completely unspoilt and remote, and you could only reach it by a long walk over Customs Pass and round the flanks of Razor Hill, or by taking the funny little ferry boat which left Shaukiwan every morning and chugged its leisurely way to Hang Hau. Deck space was small, and the passengers, a cheerful crowd of country folk, perched themselves on a mixed cargo of rice bags and household goods, and even on one occasion a coffin—whether occupied or not we did not enquire. And there was always a jolly bustle on arriving at Hang Hau; the sampans swooped around the launch like a flock of starlings, and unless you were careful you would find your pack snatched from your hand and yourself bundled into a boat and rowed off to some village on the wrong side of the bay. But nowadays we rush out to Hang Hau at forty miles an hour, and as likely as not find the bathing beach crowded.

High Junk Peak is only a little hill, but one which has given me some very happy memories. Its airy ridge forms the backbone of the peninsula, with Junk Bay on one side and Port Shelter on the other, and its pointed summit commands a magnificent view. Mere size is not everything in a mountain, and if you can reach such a delightful viewpoint after a scramble of only a few hundred feet, so much the better. The summit can be reached most quickly from the road above Clear Water Bay, but if you prefer a longer walk you can leave the road about half a mile beyond Hang Hau, and climb the hillside to the south; this brings you on to the ridge a mile north of the summit of High Junk Peak. Cattle are put to graze up here; the turf is short and springy, and you can stride along over the dips and rises of that exhilarating ridge without fear of twisting an ankle—

abiding citizens are forced to live in the city. Perhaps the piercing wind is the punishment.

The ridge walk from Sheung Yeung Shan (Upper Sheep Hill) to High Junk Peak has retained its exhilarating character. It's a splendid outing, which can be continued down to Tin Ha Shan (Lower Fields Hill) and Joss House Bay. There's an odd notice at 196690 warning you not to jump off the cliffs; it has a cartoon showing what happens if you do. On the west side of the ridge between High Junk Peak and Tin Ha Shan, there are some curious stone enclosures; purpose unknown to me, but intriguing.

As I was striding along the tops, I wondered about some of the place-names in this area. Junk Bay, Junk Island, High Junk Peak. Why is there so much junk around? Or do they commemorate the old-style Chinese boats? In fact, none of the Chinese names has anything to do with either junk or junks. Junk Bay is the General's Bay. Junk Island is Buddhist Temple Island. High Junk Peak is the Old Man Fishing.

The General, according to local legend, was a member of the imperial staff helping the Song emperor escape from the Mongols. He is said to have had a lookout on Ap Tsai Wan, the headland north of Hang Hau village, but that sounds odd to me because he wouldn't have had much of a view out to sea. Much better if it had been on the headland south of Hang Hau.

Nearly two square miles of Junk Bay has been newly reclaimed in order to accommodate one of Hong Kong's new towns. Many of the people evicted from the Kowloon Walled City are being rehoused here. On the western side of the bay is Rennie's Mill (Suicide Ridge). Rennie was a Canadian who set up a flour mill out here, but went bankrupt and hung himself. Since the 1949 Revolution it's been a stronghold for Nationalist supporters who fled from the Communists but didn't go to Taiwan.

Tung Lung Island is worth a visit if you can get there (by gaido from Sai Wan). There's a Qing dynasty fort, built in 1720 to deter pirates, now clearly visible from the mainland with a tarpaulin cover to protect it from the elements. I can't imagine it was very effective, stuck out on this isolated island with only 25 soldiers stationed here until it was abandoned in 1810. This and other similar forts are described in *Forts and Pirates*.

Tung Lung Island also has the largest of Hong Kong's nine rock carvings, somewhere by the shore a mile west of the fort. This was referred to in the 1819 *Gazetteer*; perhaps one of the soldiers discovered it while out rambling. It's been tentatively dated to the Bronze Age, between 1200–200 B.C., by 20th century archaeologists like Bill Meacham, who speculated about this and Hong Kong's other examples in *Rock Carvings in Hong Kong*, a booklet published in 1976 by the Tao Fung Shan Christian Centre.

Meacham's booklet mentions more rock carvings in this area, behind the Tin Hau Temple at Joss House Bay, which the press nicknamed 'pirate maps' when they

a rare pleasure in Hong Kong. The ridge ends with a steep little climb up to the cairn on the summit of the peak, reached in less than an hour from Hang Hau.

From the top you look straight down into the green shallows of Clear Water Bay. Beyond are the Ninepins, their cliffs encircled by fringes of white foam, and away to the north-west stand our old friends Ma On Shan and Buffalo Hill, seen to advantage from here. The cliff on the east face of High Junk Peak can be climbed from its base direct up to the cairn, but it is not recommended to enthusiastic rock climbers; the cliff springs from almost impenetrable scrub, and although the rocks are comparatively sound and excitingly steep every ledge is covered with treacherous grass.

If you descend to the south side of the peak, you can return to your starting point either along the road, or along a path which crosses the western slopes of the ridge high above Junk Bay.

Clear Water Bay is better known to launch picnickers than to walkers. It well deserves its popularity, for it is, I think, the most beautiful of all Hong Kong's beaches. A lover of solitude does well to avoid it on summer week-ends, but there is some grand country around it where he will be alone with the Kites and perhaps a Sea Eagle. From the fork in the road above Clear Water Bay there is a rough path leading off to the right, and skirting round the bushy hillside a few hundred feet above the farther beach. It will take you out on to the high ground farther along the peninsula to the south of High Junk Peak, and continues around the base of the round-topped hill known as Tin Ha Shan to Joss House Bay at the end of the peninsula.

Every year, on the third day of the third moon, the temple at Joss House Bay is the scene of a great concourse of boats of all kinds, which come from miles up and down the coast, and I believe that the festival is well worth visiting, though I have never done so myself. The boat people come in hundreds to worship the goddess Tin Hau, Daughter of Heaven, who is the guardian deity of seafarers. The temple itself is a picturesque building, of no great distinction, standing among the trees on a walled terrace overlooking the beach. Inside it, besides the usual temple trappings,

Rock Worship

Every culture has sacred objects. Scattered all over Hong Kong's hills are rocks which local people believe can influence their destiny:

The rough, barren, mountainous country I have described, has given birth to many superstitions and legends. Some of the huge stones on the hill sides are supposed to represent the tiger, the dragon, and the phoenix. The stones on some hills are said to have locomotive powers, and to pursue any adventurous traveller who attempts to mount their sides; other stones are said, when touched, to have the power of producing pains in the stomach, and others to emit white vapours from their surface.

'A Notice of the Sanon District', by the Rev Mr
Krone, read before the China Branch of the
Royal Asiatic Society, 24 February 1858.
Reprinted in *JHKBRAS*, Volume 7, 1967.

By no means all rocks are as malignant as those that Krone described. Many are benign, and are worshipped regularly by women (and some-times by men) needing a bit of extra help with marriage and children. In Chinese Creeds and Customs *(South China Morning Post Ltd., 1953–8), V. R. Burkhardt noted that: 'As the emblem of fertility, of paramount importance in a race devoted to ancestral worship, they receive their tribute from engaged couples whose duty it is to ensure the perpetua-tion of the clan.'*

The two most famous stones in Hong Kong are Lover's Rock on Bowen Road and Amah Rock above Sha Tin. Investigating Lover's Rock, Hugh Baker concluded that it was of purely phallic significance. He writes in More Ancestral Images *(South China Morning Post Ltd., 1980):*

Alas! As seems nearly always to be the case, when I had come to this immaculate and very satisfactory explanation, a great tide of doubt nearly submerged it. I spoke to an old woman who makes a living by undertaking the complex rituals for worshippers who come to the rock—she surely must understand what it is about? "Why do people come here to worship?" I asked artlessly and in full certainty of what the answer would be. "Oh, to pray for wealth, of course", she said, shattering my innocent faith. And so they do, as well as to pray for husbands and children, for connubial bliss, for scholastic success . . . for curing of illness, and for relief from persistent ill luck.

With these all-embracing reasons, rocks are just one aspect of the eclectic Chinese approach that tries to cover all bets. Buddha and Tin Hau, Kwun Yam and Wong Tai Sin, the Earth God and the sacred rock— one of them is bound to come up with the goods, so you go to them all. Each one has its own particular virtues and applications. Each one has its own story, and there are always different versions of the tales

Continued on page 75

are two big models of junks; on the deck of each junk is a most amusing little house, with a very un-nautical resemblance to a country cottage, within which a little man, presumably the master of the junk, sits in solitary state.

Half a mile over the hill behind Joss House Bay is the diminutive fishing harbour of Po To Au, opening on to Clear Water Bay. It is very small and very beautiful; looking down from above on the tiny harbour, with its village and temple and anchored boats, the scene has all the exquisite charm of a miniature. I think that when I retire I shall go and live at Po To Au, and keep a small sailing boat, and amuse myself by catching lobsters when I am not too busy looking at the view.

Sharp Peak and Fung Bay. Mention has already been made of the Sai Kung road, constructed by the Japanese. It leaves the Clear Water Bay road on the north-east side of Razor Hill, and leads around Hebe Haven to the fishing village of Sai Kung. It is a steep and narrow road; one-way traffic is in force, and cars require a police permit to use it.

Not far to the north of Sai Kung is the narrow isthmus joining the second of the three peninsulas to the mainland. The peninsula is an extensive stretch of wild hilly country, almost surrounded by sea, with Port Shelter to the south, Mirs Bay to the east, and Tolo Channel to the north; its outlying parts are accessible only by boat. At the eastern end, jutting out into Mirs Bay, is Sharp Peak, also known as Fung Peak (1,520 feet). It is a fine upstanding mountain, whose rocky spire looks a good deal higher than it really is, and it had long been an ambition of mine to climb it. The opportunity came one summer, when, through the kindness of some friends, a launch called at Long Harbour, not far from the foot of the peak.

It was a showery day in July, and our mountain, thinly veiled in falling rain, looked tremendously imposing as we drew near. The storm caught us while we were being rowed ashore, and it was a very bedraggled and disreputable gang that stepped on to the beach at Tan Ka Wan. At any rate we were pleasantly cool. A walk of a mile or so over a low pass and along a

behind these sacred rocks. One of the most delightful I have come across is in a 1938 book that I bought at a jumble sale, Hong Kong *by E. Thorbecke:*

At Sha Tin in the New Territories the soft line of green hills is strangely broken by one crowned with a boulder which is shaped like a Chinese woman carrying a child on her back. The boat people know the story of this monument built by nature's giant hand and they firmly believe in it.

Once upon a time there was a young fisherman who lived on a junk with his pretty young wife and their baby son. They were happy together and content with their work which gave them a living in the beautiful surroundings of the bays and hills.

One night the young fisherman had a dream. A fairy appeared to him in rays of gold and purple and told him to go to the South to Kwangsi, where he would find wealth and happiness. But if he disobeyed, misery would come over his family and himself.

The fisherman woke with a start. Darkness wrapped the world and the young man comforted himself that it had just been a dream haunting him in his slumber. As soon as he fell asleep again, however, the same dream ordered him to go away to Kwangsi or punishment would befall him.

Three times he dreamt the same dream. In the morning he went to see the fortune-teller and asked his advice. The fortune-teller looked up the books of the classics and sought in the stars for the meaning of these dreams. At last he confirmed that those mystic orders had to be obeyed.

The young wife wept bitterly when her husband set forth to meet his destiny. With her child on her back she climbed the hill and waved good-bye as long as she could see the small junk vanishing into the purple and golden rays of the sunset. Day after day she climbed the hill and looked out where her husband had gone. Day after day her anxiety grew and her longing for him became unbearable. Longer and longer she stayed every day, searching for the junk which might bring back her child's father and her happiness.

But he never returned. She waited and waited until she turned into stone. There she will wait through eternity, upright, her face turned towards the empty bay from where a small junk sailed an eternity ago.

In homage to similar expressions of devotion, local people have visited sacred rocks for hundreds of years. Perhaps the women would discover them on their grass-cutting trips, have lunch there, and then revisit them when good luck seemed to follow. Now that grass is no longer cut, visits to the hills are much less regular, and most local people get no closer to the tops of the hills than the sacred rocks.

rocky foreshore brought us to the foot of Sharp Peak. The north face of the mountain, which rose steeply above us, was obviously a difficult climb, so we walked up to the pass to the right of the peak, from which the summit was easily reached by a steep scramble up the south-west ridge.

The party was in high spirits, the weather was clearing up, and the view was glorious; altogether it was a good moment when we stepped on to the top of the most remote and inaccessible of the Hong Kong mountains. We sat there watching the showers sweeping long skirts of rain across the hills on the far side of Mirs Bay, and we speculated on the activities of the people living in the little villages tucked away in recesses of the hills below us; they looked peaceful enough, but they have a bad reputation for smuggling and piracy on a small scale.

The sun came out as we walked down; it really is too hot for energetic mountain-climbing in July, and when we slipped gratefully into the sea on our return to Tan Ka Wan, the water almost seemed to sizzle at the touch of our sunburnt limbs. We splashed for long in its blessed coolness before climbing on board the launch. The trip home, steaming up the long reaches of Tolo Channel towards the setting sun, was one of the loveliest that I remember.

Fung Bay, a mile to the south of Sharp Peak, possesses a fine stretch of sand; it faces the open sea, and during the N.E. monsoon big rollers break on the beach. I once visited it; an expedition which is amusing to look back on, though it was rather too strenuous at the time. We started late, for the auxiliary engine of the yacht had broken down on the way to Rocky Harbour. We lost our way over the hills, and it was not until 4 p.m. that we reached Fung Bay, where we could not resist a bathe in those tumultuous breakers. Night fell when we were still miles from the yacht, and for two hours we stumbled in darkness, wind and rain, along a pathless coast, too weary even to swear. But this was not all; when the boat returned to Hang Hau, where our cars were awaiting us, it was too rough for the dinghy to ferry us ashore, and we had to plunge once more into the dark unfriendly sea and swim for it.

were found in 1974. Meacham, however, dismisses them with the comment that they are totally different in character from all the others. I've wandered around the area looking for them, but there's no sign of where they might be.

There are, however, signs to a famous rock which still bears the thoughts of an official who was stationed at Kowloon City during the Song dynasty, around the time that the first Chinese farmers were settling in the Hong Kong area. The AD 1274 inscription is translated in various books, and the Antiquities and Monuments Office has just issued an excellent leaflet on the carving and the temple. Lo Hsiang-lin also tells the story of how they are connected with a family from Tai Hom Tsuen, a tiny village next to Wong Tai Sin, in Kowloon.

Tin Hau, an extraordinary sea goddess, has two dozen temples in Hong Kong. She was originally a fisherman's daughter in the early Song dynasty, around AD 1000, and lived for only 27 years. But in those few years she acquired a reputation for miraculous powers (such as being able to skim across the water on a flimsy straw mat with no sail—which sounds as though she invented surfboarding) and filial piety (she saved her father from drowning). If Graham had visited Joss House Bay for the festival, he would have gone on the wrong day; it is on the twenty-third day of the third month, not the third day.

Po To Au, now spelt Po Toi O, looks idyllic from above. The fishy smell that lingers over the inlet only hits you as you walk down the road that has been built since the war.

Impressive sea cliffs encircle Tung Lung Island and the southern end of the peninsula, but these are not for amateurs. One of the named climbs on Fat Tong Kok, just below the clubhouse, is called Cannonball Buttress, because on the first ascent, a rusty pirate cannonball was found embedded in the cliff.

The barrier to motor traffic on the Sai Kung Road now lies 10 miles to the north-east, at Tai Lam Chung, where a large carpark gets completely jammed on sunny weekends. The queues for buses back to town in the afternoon are phenomenal—you only need to see those once, and you'll immediately start planning your walks to ensure that you don't end up here.

Sharp Peak (in Chinese, something like Locust and Snake Peak) is now accessible to anyone with a few dollars for the bus fare, a good pair of legs, and the imagination to travel so far. Just as in Graham's day, the journey from town to the start of the climb takes longer than the walk itself. In its isolated position, Sharp Peak stands out more clearly than the clutch of hills to its west, of which more later.

There are three approaches to Sharp Peak. Most walkers come over from Pak Tam Au via Chek Keng, along the Maclehose Trail. But if you were walking up the coast from the south, you could climb the south-east ridge, or go round to the east ridge over Tung Wan Shan (East Bay Hill) and Mai Fan Teng (Ground Rice Top). The third approach is to follow Graham along the coast; this is still on my 'next summer' list. The final scramble to the summit up the south-west ridge

In the sea inlets around the country described in this chapter you can watch all the different methods of fishing practised in Hong Kong. Most of the population in this district gain their livelihood from the sea, whether they be the crews of the big three-masted fishing junks, or small boys poking sea-urchins off the rocks with a stick.

The junks may be at sea for days at a time, and any traveller in an ocean-going ship will have seen the fishing fleets at work far out of sight of land. Sometimes the boats trawl in pairs, and sometimes they work singly with a net supported on a long boom over the gunwale. A big fishing junk is a lovely sight, as is any other thing that has been built for centuries by craftsmen; the cut of her sails and the lines of her hull are obviously traditional designs, handed down from generation to generation of skilled boat builders. She can stand up to any weather except a typhoon, and her crew are magnificent seamen.

Many of the sampans fish at night, with the aid of acetylene flares which attract the fish. Another method, used in shallower water, is to spread a long net in a semi-circle between two boats, while a third rows towards it, the crew drumming on the thwarts with wooden sticks; the noise scares the fish into the net, which is then closed and drawn inboard. Explosives, obtained illegally from quarrymen, are sometimes used by the sampan people. The fuse of a stick of dynamite is cut short, and the stick is thrown as a bomb, timed to explode almost as soon as it touches the water. Any fish in the vicinity are killed or stunned by the explosion, and can easily be netted. It is a dangerous game, and there are many serious accidents.

Fishing stakes are a familiar sight around the shores of the Colony. They generally consist of four sloping poles supporting the corners of a large net, the whole contraption being raised or lowered by means of a primitive winch on shore. After the net has been raised the catch is shaken out into a waiting sampan through a funnel-shaped hole in the middle of the net. There are some big fishing stakes of this sort standing in fairly deep water in the middle of Tolo Channel, worked from thatched huts constructed on poles over the water.

Photo. H. Hubert

High Junk Peak and Hang Hau

Near Tai Po you may see a sampan moored in shallow water, with a man standing in it and poking about on the bottom with a pair of bamboo poles perhaps fifteen feet long. They are the handles of a kind of gigantic tongs, with which he is feeling for shellfish.

In the days of the Tang dynasty, and for some hundreds of years after, Tai Po was one of the Imperial pearl fisheries. It is said that the pearl divers were sent down tied to a weighted rope, and were pulled up again only when the boatmen above thought it was time for them to have some air; a barbarous practice. Oyster fishing is still carried on in Deep Bay, on the other side of the New Territories.

Besides all the boat people, there are legions of humble folk who fish from the shore with rod and line, or go out with sticks and baskets to collect shellfish of various kinds from the mud-flats and rocks.

from Nam She Au is exhilarating. It's one of the few places in Hong Kong where you do have to take your hands out of your pockets, and use them to assist your legs and keep your balance. That last 100 metres is worth the long trek up. And when you get your breath back and examine the view, you can't but help be grateful that the effort is so richly rewarded.

In front of you, to the north and east, is the South China coast. The groups of mountains behind the coast are visible all the way round to Pao Gou Ling (Throwing Dog Ridge) and Jian Feng Ding (Sharp Peak Top, surely an overkill of descriptive words), almost due east on the other side of Mirs Bay. Beyond there is Daya Bay, where China is constructing a nuclear power station.

Nine miles north, only two miles from the Chinese shore, is the flat island of Ping Chau, rather oddly made part of Hong Kong's New Territories by the 1898 Lease. I'm told that Ping Chau is a grand destination for a weekend trip. Although it looks flat from a distance, it actually has some spectacular coastal cliffs and rocks.

Looking further round, to the west, words fail me. All the Sai Kung hills seem to be at our feet, and behind them is a splendid backdrop. The Plover Cove hills and Pat Sin Leng, with Robin's Nest and Ng Tung Shan behind them; the whole length of the range from Ma On Shan south to Kowloon Peak, and from there south to High Junk Peak, and behind them all the mass of Tai Mo Shan; maybe even glimpses of Tai To Yan and Kai Keung Leng; Mount Parker, and the Hong Kong hills to the southwest, and even beyond there the triple peaks of Lantau. This sort of view is a reason to climb hills.

In the early 1990's, smuggling is again in the headlines. Here on the eastern end of Sai Kung, and also on the far western end of Lantau, stocks of consumer goods (TVs, videos, electronics, luxury cars), are shipped off to China on huge speedboats that travel five times faster than the old Naval Police vessels that are supposed to stop them.

In one incident, a Hong Kong police launch in Tolo Harbour was circled by what they identified as a smugglers' boat, and chasing it a Chinese police boat. As the two other vessels roared off towards China, the police radioed for a helicopter which came and took photos. Responding to an official protest about their presence so far inside Hong Kong waters, the Chinese denied all knowledge of the incident, prompting speculation that they were protecting the smugglers and that the chase had been a decoy to cover up their role.

Just a few miles north is Tap Mun Chau, or Grass Island, another popular Sunday destination. The ferry chugs up from Wong Shek Pier in Long Harbour.

Tai Long Wan (Big Wave Bay), which Graham called Fung Bay, is almost unique in not needing a squad of attendants to come and clean up on Monday mornings— worth visiting for that alone. Even on remote hillsides I often come across bottles and cans, food wrappers, and even neatly wrapped plastic bags full of rubbish, just tossed

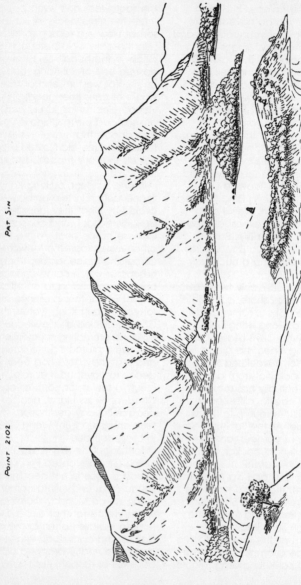

POINT 2102

PAT SIN

The Pat Sin Range and Plover Cove from the South

casually to one side of the path, miles from nowhere. Do the vandals who desecrate our countryside like this think that someone is walking after them to pick up their litter?

The Maclehose Trail comes along the edge of the bay from the south, and then heads inland over the pass and down to Chek Keng. After a long slow steady climb from there to Pak Tam Au, the would-be Trail-walker is faced with a heart-breaking flight of steps up 300 metres. They do end, despite all rational convictions to the contrary, when they reach the ridge of Ngau Yee Shek Shan and the well-concealed plateau centred on Cheung Sheung. In Chinese, Ngau Yee Shek Shan means the Hill of the Bull's Ear Rock. In old ceremonies marking an alliance, the prince would hold a plate containing the ears of a sacrificial bull, and from this came a phrase meaning 'to be the acknowledged leader'. There's probably a rock looking like a plate with bull's ears on it, but after climbing up from Pak Tam Au, I've never had the energy to go looking.

This plateau is invisible except from the hills above—looking up from any direction below, you wouldn't know it existed. With its ideal location, it became a wartime centre for resistance to the Japanese occupying forces. Now it's only a drinks stop and a camp site, and a grazing ground for cattle indifferent to its past.

The hills of Sai Kung offer some delightful walking. To be sure, they are nearly all separated by deep valleys; and yes, getting from one top to its neighbour is hard work, especially in summer. But your efforts are repaid by constantly-changing panoramas. This is now the most popular recreation area in Hong Kong.

From Mount Hallowes (which has two Chinese names—Carrying Firewood Hill, and Great Basket Lid) in the north to High Island (Grain Ship Bay) in the south. From Kai Kung Shan (Rooster Hill) in the west to Mai Fan Teng in the east. And in the centre, gems like Lui Ta Shek (Thunderstruck Rock) and Tin Mei Shan (Farm End Hill).

And so many valleys between them. There's the mysteriously-named 'Stone Trail' and the waterfalls in the woods by Luk Wu. The walk along the valley from Tai Mong Tsai to Ping Tun. The old village Folk Museum at Sheung Yiu. Jacob's Ladder, giving access to Cheung Sheung from Three Fathoms Cove. The Drumming Rock on the beach at Hoi Ha.

The last hill in this area I climbed was Tai Tun (Big Mound), north of the road between Tai Mong Tsai and Pak Tam Chung. From the main road, you can see a steeply overhanging crag on the north-western ridge of this hill. It intrigued me for years, and whenever I went past I always vowed to check it out sometime.

When I did, I discovered a terrific view from the summit, and a crag overlooking two 30-foot slabs, all regularly used by the Outward Bound School. I walked down through charming woods below the crags (but I doubt if I could find a way up) and spent an hour lazing by the stream in the valley, basking in afternoon sunshine after a hard morning run.

CHAPTER VII.

BETWEEN TOLO HARBOUR AND STARLING INLET.

The range of hills which stretches from Tai Po far out into Mirs Bay is one of the most attractive districts in the Colony, and the least spoilt; long may it remain untouched. It has a distinct character of its own; this may be partly due to the nature of the underlying rock, which is not exclusively granite, but contains some shaley red sandstone. In place of the usual hummocky hills, with their boulder-strewn slopes and rocky outcrops, there is a long sweeping escarpment comprising the Pat Sin range and its continuation eastward. The ridge falls away very steeply on its south side to the waters of Tolo Harbour, and slopes gently to the north in rolling moorlands and wooded valleys towards Starling Inlet and Sha Tau Kok; there are places here where you might almost imagine yourself to be in the Welsh uplands. The whole range forms a splendid background to the view across Tolo Harbour from the Tai Po road—surely one of the loveliest you will see from any road in the world.

Sha Lo Tung. The shortest and easiest walk in the district is from Tai Po to Kwanti, crossing the range by the Sha Lo Tung pass. The distance is about 6 miles, the climb to the pass is not at all arduous, and the scenery is superb; an admirable walk if the clouds are low, or you are not feeling too energetic. Starting from the bridge at Tai Po Market, the path winds along the north shore of Tolo Harbour. The first village on the left suffered terribly in the disastrous tidal wave which swept across all the low ground near Tai Po and Shatin during the typhoon of September 2nd, 1937. About a mile and a half from the road the path crosses a stream; a few yards beyond the bridge, in a little wood, another path branches off to the left climbing the hillside at an easy gradient to the head of a valley to the north. It is a lovely place, particularly in spring; the paddy fields below, all in their freshest green, are encircled by deep woods, where you may hear the notes of Koels, Barbets and Golden Orioles. The path crosses the gap between Cloudy Hill and the Pat Sin range; at its highest point, as on so many of the passes in the New Territories, an old pine tree used to stand as a landmark. Sha Lo Tung village lies a little way down on

Commentary—Chapter 7

GRAHAM would still feel at home in this north-eastern corner of Hong Kong. True, Plover Cove has been turned into a huge freshwater reservoir on the southern side, and a road now goes from Tai Po along the coast before heading north to the Sha Tau Kok Road. But people mostly leave this area alone, preferring places which are nearer the city and easier to reach. Away from the road, among the rolling moorlands and wooded valleys, there is little sign of the progress and change that has transformed the rest of Hong Kong. This, I think, is where I would bring Graham if he could somehow spend one more day on his hills.

The sheltered valley that contains Sha Lo Tung village is at risk. A private developer bought all the village land a few years ago and threatened to build Spanish villas unless he was allowed to buy a big chunk of country park and construct a golf course, where he said he would allow the public to play occasionally. The government did a secret deal with him, which was exposed in 1991. Legal action by Friends of the Earth and other environmental groups has stopped him for the moment. Although the government is supposed to act as the public's watchdog, some government departments actually seem to want to help the developer ruin this beautiful valley at taxpayers' expense, so the environmental groups are having to be the vigilantes instead. Nearly all of Graham's walk is now paved, but it still goes through some lovely

country, and is worth revisiting before it's too late. The Ting Kok Road traces the 1938 coastline, and you can take a bus or taxi from Tai Po market to the Fung Yuen turn-off.

All the flat land which you pass on the right is reclaimed. Where does the fill come from? From all around you. West of Fung Yuen, there used to be a 110 metre high hill—it's almost disappeared. Other hills around the coast have been 'skinned': had the top ten or twenty metres taken off before being re-seeded.

North of Sha Lo Tung, the winding valley is now home to Hok Tau Reservoir, which is quite discreet and almost adds to the charm. The hill named Tai Leng Pei (Big Ridge Skin) on our map was called 'Gib' on Graham's; its shape obviously reminded the British troops of the Rock of Gibraltar. 'Gib' is easy to climb and gives an expansive view over the northern part of the New Territories.

Cloudy Hill (Nine Dragon Pit Hill) makes a good half-day walk. It can be climbed from north-west (Bird's Pass), south-west (Ying Pun Ha), east (Sha Lo Tung) or north-east (Hok Tau). I've done it as an extra to Pat Sin Leng, but that's a bit of a stretch. Nestling in the arms of the south-west ridge is Hong Lok Yuen, a private housing estate built on the site of a bandit warlord's old hideaway. Bird's Hill (Dragon's Hill in Chinese) is a sporting little scramble from Bird's Pass; a nice way of following a walk over Cloudy Hill and, like 'Gib', a fine vantage point for the northern New Territories.

Pat Sin Leng is properly the name for only the eastern end of the

the far side of the pass; the path continues northward by the headwaters of a stream and down a long winding valley, eventually reaching the Sha Tau Kok road near Kwanti racecourse. Time, about 2½ hours from Tai Po. The return journey can be made by bus to Fanling, and so home by train.

Cloudy Hill. This modest hill, 1,440 feet high, may easily be reached from Tai Po market. The route described in the preceding paragraph is followed as far as the pass to the south of Sha Lo Tung, whence the ridge to the left will lead to the summit in some 2 hours from Tai Po. A track down the airy south ridge affords a pleasant route back to the starting point.

The Pat Sin Ridge. *Pat Sin* is translated as "eight fairies", and is said to refer to the eight immortals of Taoist mythology. The range stretches from Sha Lo Tung to Plover Cove, and at its eastern end are the eight hummocks from which it takes its name. The western end of the ridge may be climbed from Sha Lo Tung. Heading north-eastward from the village, the path crosses a few paddy fields and some low hillocks to the little hamlet of Ping Shan Tsai, encircled by an amphitheatre of great hills. Wild lilies grow well in the upper part of this valley. A track leads up the hillside behind the village, bending to the left round the edge of a spur and into the upper part of the corrie behind. The track then follows the watercourse up to its source on the northern side of the ridge. From here it is a short scramble to the edge of the scarp, where you find yourself unexpectedly looking down the precipitous southern face on the paddy fields bordering Tolo Harbour.

It is a good district for flowers; in summer the ridge is covered with bamboo orchids, in such profusion of bloom as I have rarely seen in the Colony. And at the foot of the hills to the north the pastures at Easter time are starred with a little blue gentian; I always think it is particularly charming of this gentian to grow in Hong Kong, for it reminds me of flowery meadows in the Alps.

ridge; the highest point in the centre is called Wong Leng (Yellow Ridge), and the backdrop to Ping Shan Tsai (Flat Hill Village) in the west is Ping Fung Shan (Windshelter Hill). At Tai Mei Tuk Visitor Centre you can learn all about the Eight Immortals and identify each hummock. Both ridges at the western end are good ascents; the route up Ping Fung Shan is the easier of the two to locate and follow.

Pat Sin Leng is very popular, and Graham's notes are still perfectly adequate. Just one point: climb all the humps. Otherwise, how will you have any chance of attaining immortality? One of the eight immortals, Ho Hsien Ku, did it by eating powdered stones; another, Ts'ao Kuo Chiu, a Song Emperor's brother-in-law, did it by going to the mountains as a hermit. This is your chance. The simplest way to descend from the eastern end is to go north, turn right a few hundred yards below the summit, and traverse south to reach Tai Mei Tuk.

Graham's Tai Lek Teng Hill is Kwai Tau Leng (Tortoise Head Hill). There are good tracks up Kwai Tau Leng from Tan Chuk Hang to the west, and Nam Chung to the north-east. North of Kwai Tau Leng there's a flat ridge about 250 metres high and half a mile long, called Wa Shan (Flower Hill) by the locals, like the mountain Hua Shan in Shaanxi province that's sacred for Taoists. Wa Shan can be reached from either end, but the paths are badly overgrown, and hard to follow. The tracks to the sides don't exist. I once had to spend a night out in winter on top of the north-east end of Wa Shan, within hearing distance of the villages below, but unable to find a way down. Since then, I've been up the path from Hoi Pui Leng, only to miss it on my way down a few minutes later, even in full daylight.

That overnight bivouac was chastening. It happened one Sunday in December after orienteering at Luk Keng and a late lunch on the 121-metre hill. I climbed Kwai Tau Leng, admired the view, and located the path down the north face—thoroughly overgrown, but clearly improving further down and along the ridge. Give it a go, I resolved; still two hours before dusk. I struggled through the bushes down to the ridge, and trotted easily along, watching on my left for the path down to Sheung Wo Hang. No sign of it; the north-western slope is thickly wooded. No problem, I'll take the path on my right and go down to Cheng Uk. No sign of it. I went down a bit; still no sign of it, but the houses are only 400 yards away. With barely half an hour of daylight left, I had to find a way through somehow, so I started pushing at the bushes. Bushes became thick jungle; pushing became panicky thrashing.

Then I recalled the news item in November about the human bones found in a remote Sai Kung valley, and realised it was too risky to have an accident where I was: my bones would never be found. Conceding that discretion was the better part of valour, I struggled back to the ridge and carried on to the end with hopes of finding the path down to Hoi Pui Leng. No sign of it.

A rough track follows the curving edge of the scarp eastward to its highest point (2,102 feet), reached in 3 hours from Tai Po. From here it is possible to descend to Tolo Harbour by a prominent spur to the south of the summit.

The Pat Sin range may also be tackled from the Sha Tau Kok road on the north-west side; this route is quicker and just as attractive as the approach from Tai Po and Sha Lo Tung already described. Leaving the Sha Tau Kok road 2½ miles from the Fanling cross-roads, a path crosses the level cultivated ground for about a mile south-eastward to a small village at the foot of Tai Lek Teng Hill. (On the 1:80,000 map, this village is about ¼ inch west of the T of Tai). The path climbs the hillside behind the village, bending right-handed to the saddle between Tai Lek Teng and the Pat Sin range. From here a track may be found up a gently sloping rib leading to the main ridge to the west of the highest point.

The ridge stretches a long way east of the summit, but it will well repay an energetic party to traverse its whole length to the outstanding bluff which overlooks the Bride's Pool, descending thence either to Plover Cove or to Sha Tau Kok. Eastward of the highest point the track follows the edge of the scarp for about a mile to the first of the eight humps of the Pat Sin. I hardly think you will want to climb all the remaining humps; the track dodges most of them on the northern side. From the eighth it is possible to make almost a bee-line down the mountain-side and across country to the head of Starling Inlet, where the Sha Tau Kok road is regained. Most of this route is along a shelf of high ground between the Pat Sin and the valleys to the north-east, commanding wide views over a very lovely stretch of country.

The Bride's Pool. The easiest way to reach this delectable spot is to go by sea from Tai Po to Plover Cove, whence a walk of less than a mile will bring you to the pool. But the trip takes too long by sampan, and not many of us are fortunate enough to obtain the services of a launch at Tai Po.

What to do? I didn't have a torch with me, and there was no way I'd be able to retrace my steps without light. The inevitable conclusion as dusk fell was that I'd have to stay where I was until dawn came to my rescue. Nothing like that had ever happened to me before, but as a matter of routine I always carry bivouac gear, emergency food and water, and a First Aid kit. Thirteen hours later I got up and started back the way I'd come. It took two-and-a-half hours to reach a phone. My girlfriend, bless her, had called my boss at 5.00 in the morning to ask for help. One of my orienteering friends, a senior police officer, had notified the search division, but as he said: 'Policy is to wait until 10.00 a.m. Too many times we've gone looking for people, only to find that they spent the night safely with a lady in Mong Kok. It doesn't do to panic.' I agreed, half-heartedly wishing that I *had* been in Mong Kok.

I received two suggestions to avoid the problem. Prohibit solo walking, or make solo walkers carry mobile phones or walkie talkies. Neither idea would work, but I learned three lessons. Always carry a torch, no matter how certain you are that you won't be out after dark. Always leave a note of your route, so that rescuers know where to start. And always, always, always be prepared for the worst.

The delectable Bride's Pool is accessible now to all and sundry, and they certainly go there. If peace and quiet by a tranquil pool is your desire, then this is not your destination. But it is a lovely spot, and can be combined with a walk from the Sha Tau Kok side over the delightful rolling country which British troops nicknamed the Cotswolds.

Sha Tau Kok is out of bounds to anyone who doesn't live in the Closed Border Area or have legitimate business there. However, you don't have to go that far, and Graham's directions are fine for the start. Yim Tso Ha, on your right as you walk down towards Luk Keng from the main road, is a haven for egrets—A Chau (Crow Island) is full of them.

There are many tracks over the hills between Luk Keng and Bride's Pool. The main track is not clear from the old map, but I think from Graham's description it must have been the path from Chan Uk to the Monument. The crowds at Bride's Pool may deter you from bathing, but you can reliably count on having company for lunch. The village above the fall to which Graham refers is Wu Kau Tang. The path beside the Dragon's Pool retraces the footsteps of Imperial messengers.

The journey back to Tai Po should be quicker than it was in Graham's day, and dusk is not likely to leave the modern traveller stranded without any means of getting home.

The land east of Bride's Pool is the most exquisite left in Hong Kong. From the summit of Tsing Shan, now mapped as Tiu Tang Lung (Hanging Lantern), an all-round view of unparalleled beauty unfolds, in my opinion far excelling the view from Tai Mo Shan, Sharp Peak, or any other Hong Kong hill. These deserted valleys will reward many visits, if you can be patient enough to deal with overgrown paths and false trails.

The walk from Sha Tau Kok to Tai Po around the eastern end of the Pat Sin range well deserves its popularity, and will take you past the Bride's Pool and the Dragon's Pool. It is best to start from the Sha Tau Kok end, for the latter is rather a remote place at which to finish a day's walking, and you may miss the bus back to Fanling. Sha Tau Kok may be reached by car, or by train to Fanling and thence by bus. Alight where the road first reaches the sea, just short of the old Sha Tau Kok police station. The path follows the bund which divides the paddy fields from Starling Inlet. Here coral is brought ashore, to be fired in lime kilns which stand behind the beach.

About three quarters of a mile from the road, the path turns inland for a few hundred yards, then bends to the left through a gap in the foothills to Luk Keng village. From here it heads south-eastward, across the paddy fields and up into the hills. The pass over the watershed, which is only 400 feet above sea level, is soon gained; a little way down on the far side the path reaches the headwaters of a stream flowing southward; the valley begins to narrow, and soon you come unexpectedly to the edge of the big waterfall where the stream plunges over a cliff into the Bride's Pool below. The path passes close to the edge of the cliff, and it was here, I think, that the ill-fated bride of the legend was killed when her chair-bearers slipped. A scramble down the hillside will bring you to the deep still pool; clearly the place for a bathe and lunch. Time 2 hours from Sha Tau Kok.

Not far below the Bride's Pool a tributary stream comes in from the east; the Dragon's Pool lies in a thickly wooded gorge at the foot of another very lovely waterfall a few hundred yards up this stream. Although the place seems utterly wild and deserted, there is a village just beyond the top of the fall, and it would be highly imprudent to drink of the stream.

Continuing southward for half a mile the valley comes down to Plover Cove at Chung Mi village. For the rest of the way to Tai Po a good path follows the coast, first around the base of the big hill at the end of the Pat Sin range and then along the level paddy fields which border Plover Cove and Tolo Harbour. The whole walk from Sha Tau Kok to Tai Po is about 12 miles in

Allow time to get lost, and don't plan on getting back to Central early in time for a dressy evening out.

One walk Graham couldn't do is the Plover Cove Reservoir circuit. The visit to Bluff Head makes an irresistible adjunct to the round, even though it adds six miles to an already long day. But it really is worth it. Start from Wu Kau Tang and make your way up Ma Tau Fung (there is a slightly overgrown but passable route past an old shrine); once you get on the ridge, the track is plain all the way to Bluff Head. It's like making your way to the bows of a mighty ship, leaving first the mainland and then the islands behind on either side. By the time you reach Bluff Head, you're half-way to Ping Chau and the other side of Mirs Bay, and the views are terrific. I saw a deer on Fung Wong Wat Teng as we were returning—my first and only such sighting in Hong Kong.

There's a lot of up and down, but it's all in bursts of less than 100 metres, with no long effort required after the initial climb. Make a decision about Bluff Head when you get to Luk Wu Tung; at that point you're one-third of the way through the entire walk. With frequent rests, we did the round under ten hours. If necessary, you can walk across the dam in the dark.

Staying Out Late

Graham wasn't by any means the only one to get caught out in this part of the New Territories. 'E.A.C.', writing in the Hong Kong Sunday Herald *in February 1939, was another:*

The most comfortable hikes are those on which you find your way, catch your return train or bus, and get home in good time for a bath and dinner. I've seldom been on that kind of walk myself. Almost inevitably, about an hour after dark, I find myself miles from the nearest habitation, and prospects of getting home at all exceeding gloomy. Such was the quest for the Bride's Pool. The beer on the 12.10 train was very good, and we remembered this when struggling along the edge of Tolo Harbour hours later.

At Fanling, bound for Shautaukok, one should throw the tickets at the collector and rush for the bus. Tutored to politer methods, we handed in our tickets and the bus had gone before we could get to it. When eventually we did reach Shautaukok, we began correctly at the starting point, a little path at the spot where the road first reaches Starling Inlet, which led us to a tiny village, the only notable thing about which was the unanimous clamour of the inhabitants for cumshaw and the fact the males all wore trilby hats.

A short walk, with the path turning inland, brings one to Luk Keng. After that comes a short but fairly sharp climb into the foothills, about 400 feet, the only climb on the way to the Bride's Pool. There are two tracks, one paved, the other, a few yards further, a beaten track. The first is more correct, but on either success depends on choosing the right moment for going down into the valley.

This found, ever-narrowing, we soon came to the lovely gorge at the end of

Continued on page 93

length, but if the day is hot and the way seems long the last three miles can be avoided by taking a sampan at Shun Wan and crossing the water to Tai Po.

Many birds may be seen on this walk, particularly around the head of Starling Inlet. Here we once watched a dignified party of Grey Herons, standing solemn and motionless in the shallows, waiting for fish. Every one of the Colony's five species of Kingfisher (including the scarce Himalayan Pied Kingfisher) has been seen at one time or another near the path, and among the less common birds here are the Oriental Raven, the Jay and the Great Egret. One evening I was sitting on a hill near Sha Tau Kok when two Buzzards came overhead, soaring up in the blue sky on intersecting circles, obviously just enjoying themselves. "Look out!" one seemed to say, "you can't escape me", and he would swing round and make a vicious swoop at his companion. "Ho, can't I; missed again!" the other would reply, as he dodged away with an easy twist of his great wings. And so the game went on until they disappeared in the sunset.

Tsing Shan. Running eastward from the pass between Starling Inlet and the Bride's Pool is a delightful ridge, ending in a steep little peak named Tsing Shan, "the Green Hill". Twice I have had the good fortune to visit this ridge on sunny days in March and April, and on each occasion found a beautiful show of the common purple rhododendron, with a few bushes of the rare *R. westlandii*, having a big white flower, faintly flushed with pink and strongly scented. The last time I was there, the Swifts were rejoicing in the first warmth of spring, and we could hear the swish of their wings as they whirled past us in the sunlit air. It was altogether a memorable halt on the summit, for, besides the Swifts and the rhododendrons, there was Mirs Bay below us looking its loveliest, with its blue waters and its queer-shaped islands and with banks of white mist creeping along the northern shore.

That was the occasion when we assembled, a party of thirteen, at the far end of Plover Cove, to wait for the launch which was to take us back to Tai Po. Dusk came, but no launch; we had no food left, and all our extra clothes had been left on board, so it was rather a subdued party which reluctantly set out

which is the Dragon's Pool. The water topples over the cliff into the pool far below and then trickles down over a bed of huge boulders. A little further on is an overgrown track, curling away left from the main path, which leads to a delightful spot, another gorge even more lovely than that at the Dragon's Pool. Here too is a sparkling, foaming waterfall, surely one of the most entrancing scenes in the Colony.

The trouble comes afterwards, if you don't watch out. We rejoined the path, crossed the strong, three-span footbridge, and strode out for Plover Cove. A couple of hundred yards below the bridge one should cross the stream. There is a path, cleverly concealed, going sharply down the hillside to a point where the stream is spanned by boulders. We found it not and continued until we agreed we were on the wrong side of the river.

No path was visible, and the owners of the sampans, who, emulating sharks, wanted us to employ one of them, professed ignorance of it. Ultimately we ferried across and took the route round the foreshore. At first there was firm sand; and then when light disappeared, we scrambled over rocks and boulders. Useless as it seemed to go forward, there was less profit in going back and the foreshore it continued to be. Till now we had been making good time, but the going became more and more difficult and the night more and more black. At seven we were still climbing and scrambling along the narrow ledge between the face of the cliff and the sea.

Then we turned a corner and found a long wide creek confronting us. At this point, especially in the dark, the foreshore was almost impassable. We had a vague sort of idea that Taipo ought to be near, but nothing was visible but a few flickering lights like glow-worms, the lights of a few sampans fishing in the dark. Taipo, of course, was a long way across Tolo Harbour. As we stopped to consider the position, we realised that the night had become very cold. The only solution was to shout and shout for a sampan, and this we did. After twenty minutes—it seemed like a week—we saw a tiny light making its way towards us. I waved my cigarette end as a beacon.

It took us an hour and three-quarters to get to Taipo, huddled together in the fore of the boat, cramped and frozen, and having continually to resist the efforts of the sampan-man's wife to get payment in advance. The last train, the 7.50, had long gone, but with the station still open, we were able to telephone to Kowloon for a taxi. Whilst we waited for it, we took turns smoking our last cigarette.

to walk the weary miles round the shore to Tai Po. Eventually we chartered a sampan, and rowed slowly out into the bay in the darkness. There was hardly any wind to help us, which was perhaps just as well, for besides the thirteen walkers there were three very wet dogs and three rowers on board. The stability of the sampan was seriously threatened, and we hardly dared breathe.

The lights of the launch at last appeared; we waved a lantern and raised a dismal hullabaloo. The villagers on shore put their lights out, evidently thinking that a gang of very noisy pirates was abroad, but the launch was quite indifferent to our shouts and steamed serenely past us to search the coast for the wanderers. At last they spotted us, and before long we were drinking huge cups of steaming hot tea in the welcome frowst of the cabin.

Tolo Harbour from the Tai Po Road

Photo. H. Hubert

CHAPTER VIII.

NG TUNG SHAN AND THE FRONTIER.

At the time of writing this district is out of bounds. Even before the Japanese war, walking parties occasionally got into hot water for crossing the frontier, and I was once politely turned back when half way up Ng Tung Shan by the armed home-guards of the neighbouring villages. To avoid giving the police unnecessary trouble, it is well to keep to the south of the Sha Tau Kok road and the line joining Sheung Shui and Lok Ma Chau. I hope that the following notes may be found useful at some future time.

Ng Tung Shan (3,100 feet). This fine mountain can hardly be called a Hong Kong hill, as it stands in Chinese territory; but it would be a pity to leave out all mention of it, for its foot can be reached in little over an hour from Kowloon, and although the summit is only a few feet lower than Tai Mo Shan it can easily be climbed in a day's outing. In fact an energetic friend has climbed Ng Tung Shan and Tai Mo Shan between sunrise and sunset, and toyed with the idea of taking a boat across Tide Cove and ascending Ma On Shan in the evening, to round off a good day of exercise.

The most direct way up Ng Tung Shan is to make straight for the mountain across the flat paddy fields behind Sha Tau Kok, until you reach a village at the foot of the hill. The path passes the western end of this village and slants up to the left through the wood behind. A friend and I were once warned by a villager to keep clear of this wood, as a tiger had recently killed a bullock and was supposed to be demolishing it in the undergrowth. We did not understand the warning at the time, and walked gaily through the wood without adventure. There is a tiger scare nearly every winter in some part or other of the New Territories, and there is no doubt that tigers do occasionally visit the Colony, for a man-eater was shot by the Police in 1915.

Above the wood the path bends round into a small valley between the two southern spurs of the mountain. Leave the path near the head of this valley, and climb a few hundred feet on to the shoulder of the spur to

Commentary—Chapter 8

THERE'S some very pleasant walking this side of the border. East of the KCR line is Robin's Nest and the Tsung Shan/Wa Shan ridge. West of the railway, there's Crest Hill, and the trio of hills culminating in Kai Keung Leng. Graham doesn't mention any of them, but don't be put off.

There are three ways up Robin's Nest (Safflower Ridge). The quickest is straight up the south ridge from Milestone 4. As a variation, I've tried the minor path from Man Uk Pin; it offers views of the waterfall opposite (104948) and Barker's Battery, as the valley in between was called by the army, but it's very difficult to follow now.

The second approach is up the southeast ridge from the police checkpoint and over Hung Fa Chai (Safflower Camp), which the army called Ben Nevis. On this ridge you may be stopped and questioned. I was mistaken for an illegal immigrant here; two armed Gurkhas caught me while I was perched on the summit eating lunch. They chatted for a few minutes after deciding I was harmless, and explained that they were in the middle of their ten-day duty, during which time they camp on top of the hill and watch out for suspicious characters. I found their camp later, as I was heading for the prominent 400-metre crags on the northeast ridge (120962). They prevented me from going any further because I didn't have a pass to enter the Frontier Closed Area.

A third approach with a gentler gradient is up the west ridge by the road from Miu Keng (095943); the latest edition of the map forgot the English name. You can drive up when the barrier is open, but I don't know how you'll get to it in future; a new access is being built to the Ta Kwu Ling landfill, following the route of the old main road from Sha Tau Kok to Shenzhen.

In 1789 at the tiger-infested mid-point of the old road, Buddhists built the Cheung Shan temple to provide refuge for travellers. It's still there, nestling below Wo Keng Shan. The last inhabitant, a nun from the mainland, died a few years ago aged over 90; at least she was spared the noise and dirt of construction.

A mile away in Ping Che is a temple to Tin Hau, built in 1727 by the same villagers; I guess that a vast part of the northern plain was once accessible from the sea via the Shum Chun River. At the southern end of the Ping Che Road is the Hung Shing Kung temple, which was once the main focal point for the whole community north of Tai Po. On the south side of the Sha Tau Kok Road, at 080925, is Hung Leng station, one of the halts on the old KCR branch line that closed in 1928.

All the small hills visible from Long Ridge (Tsung Shan, meaning Pine Tree Hill) have two names—important to both the farmers and the army. On Top Hill (Wa Shan, meaning Flower Hill), at the western end of the ridge, there's a 'Rain Prayer' stone from the days when rain meant life or death. It was reputedly erected by the Liu clan of Sheung Shui in 1839, when a drought threatened crops.

the right. A track follows this spur all the way up to the main ridge of the mountain, which is gained some way to the east of the summit. It is a steep climb and hard work, but the outlook is magnificent.

The top is reached in about 2½ hours from Sha Tau Kok. The view is a wide one, but rather lacks a foreground, for the tops of all the nearby hills are far below.

An alternative way from Sha Tau Kok, longer but less exhausting, is up the west ridge of the mountain. Our party followed the frontier road for about half a mile, and then crossed the paddy fields towards our first objective—a conspicuous pass on the skyline to the left of the highest point of Ng Tung Shan. We followed the stream which descends from this pass; the hills closed in around us, and soon we were zig-zagging up the steep mountain face at the head of the valley, stepping aside every now and then as the grasscutter women came down the path with their heavy loads, looking in the distance like miniature haystacks wandering on the mountain-side.

The pass was reached in 2 hours from Sha Tau Kok. We turned right and followed the ridge, which soon narrowed and rose in front of us in a very steep grassy shoulder. There was no path, and we each chose our own way up, our leader, the botanist, bounding ahead with his usual energy; whenever he looked back the rest of the party seemed to be reclining at intervals down the slope, gazing at the view in attitudes of exhaustion. Eventually, however, we all surmounted the shoulder and stepped out along the more level ridge beyond—an airy and exhilarating walk, for the crest was narrow and dropped steeply on either side. We reached the summit in 3 hours from Sha Tau Kok.

The top was covered with stunted bushes of rhododendron just coming into flower—this was in January—and we made a great botanical find, a rare and lovely magnolia, *Michelia Maudiae*, growing in a hollow nearby, with its fragrant white flowers, four inches across, in full bloom.

Walled Village, Kam Tin   *Photo. H. Hubert*

The direct route from Sha Tau Kok up the mountain, as described above, provides the easiest descent. You can take it at the double, in one swift rush down three thousand feet of mountain-side; once, with a friend who was in a hurry to get back to an evening engagement, I came down Ng Tung Shan in about 20 minutes—a great mistake.

It used to be possible to traverse Ng Tung Shan from south to north, descending on the Chinese side and returning to Hong Kong in a single day. A friend tells me that his party climbed the mountain by the ordinary way from Sha Tau Kok, went down on the north side, and eventually reached Nai Nai, a village lying about 4 miles to the west of the summit in Chinese territory. Here they caught a bus which ran from Sa Wan Hui to Shum Chun, and from Shum Chun returned by train to Kowloon.

The Frontier. From Sha Tau Kok to Sheung Shui along the frontier is a walk of about 10 miles through very attractive scenery. The road starts just short of Sha Tau Kok village, which is itself in Chinese territory, and climbs to a narrow pass under a shoulder of Ng Tung Shan. Thence it follows the headwaters of the Shum Chun river, coming down through the hills in a steep defile which gradually broadens out into the plains around Shum Chun. About a mile short of this town the road leaves the river and crosses some low hills to Sheung Shui, where it joins the New Territories road. Shum Chun itself is just as well missed, for it is not an attractive town. In lies on the Chinese side of the river; the fortress-like towers of a few pawnshops dominate the village, and nearby is the disused Casino, once much patronised by Hong Kong gamblers, and now wearing a mournful air of having seen better days.

The walk may be shortened slightly by leaving the frontier at Ta Ku Ling, and making your way south-eastward along a wide valley to Kwanti on the Sha Tau Kok road, where you can catch a bus for home.

Westward of Shum Chun the frontier continues along the river estuary to Deep Bay. The border country around Lok Ma Chau and Mai Pu is mostly marsh land, of which more in the next chapter. Between the frontier and the hills to the south is the

The British prepared elaborate defence plans for these hills, but they were useless during World War II. The Japanese invaders went right past, sweeping southwards at a pace which astonished the British. Battles for hills were fought further south, on the Gindrinkers' Line, briefly, and on Hong Kong island. Up here, rusty barbed wire is the plans' only relic.

Graham might have been Hong Kong's first prisoner of war. He was captured while checking a weather station near the border on the first day of the Japanese invasion in 1941.

I'm not sure whether Crest Hill is out of bounds or not. I walked up the restricted road from Ngam Pin one day, but was stopped near the end of the road below the summit lookout post by a soldier who told me I couldn't go any further. 'It's restricted', he said, but agreed to let me up the last few yards to enjoy the view. While I looked, we talked.

I asked him what he would have done if I'd walked up from Ho Sheung Heung and lobbed a grenade down into his lookout post from above. 'There isn't a path', he said. 'Yes, there is', I said. He finally let me through, but I discovered that the only way was by going upstairs in the lookout post and out of the back window, so I suppose he was right to stop me. The ridge path from Ho Sheung Heung is a more diplomatic approach.

Let's leave Tai To Yan, and Kai Keung Leng and the hills north of it to the next chapter.

A Wartime Picnic

Some hill-lovers tried to continue as normal during the war. Oliver Lindsay recounted a frustrated picnic in 1942 or 1943 in At the Going Down of the Sun *(Hamish Hamilton, 1981):*

Another incident which occurred concerned three neutral Danes, named Herschend, Jacobson, and Anderson, who went for a picnic in the hills near Kowloon one Sunday afternoon. They had just finished their lunch when they were pounced on by Communist guerrillas. The Danes violently protested that they had no wish to leave Hong Kong, but the Communists decided that the Danes knew too much, and so they were 'involuntarily escorted' to China where they arrived two days later in a high state of indignation.

Fanling district, a pleasant enough place but better known to the golfing and hunting fraternities than to walkers; the country here has a slightly sophisticated air, with its golf links and racecourse and week-end bungalows, and the true country lover will prefer the solitude of the hills for his rambles. There is, however, one delightful scramble which starts from Fanling; behind the railway station a path runs south-westward up a wooded hillside, leading you on to a low ridge which is a kind of subsidiary spur of the Tai Tan Yang hills. If you follow the crest of this ridge for about a mile, and turn to the left at the end of it across a narrow saddle, you will reach the upper slopes of Tai Tan Yang. It is only a short scramble to the summit where you will be rewarded by a splendid view across the green depths of the Lam Tsun valley to Tai Mo Shan standing up proudly on the far side, and really looking all of its 3,000 feet. It is an easy descent into the Lam Tsun valley, whence you can regain the Tai Po —Fanling road.

WHITE-BREASTED
KINGFISHER

Hong Kong's Fung Shui

Wutong Mountain lies 60 li to the east of the county seat. It has three fine peaks and measures several score li around. . . . At the top there is the fathomless Heavenly Pool, with many wutong trees and rare plants, and at the foot is Red Water Cave. The mountain is the dragon on which the county geomantically depends.

Peter Y.L. Ng, *New Peace County.*

Ng Tung Shan (Parasol Tree Hill) is an essential part of Hong Kong's fung shui. *Far to the north-west lie the Kunlun Mountains, home to China's most powerful dragon. Marking the northern edge of the Tibetan plateau and the southern rim of Xinjiang, the range nudges 25,000 feet at its highest and marches for a thousand miles (the same distance as Hong Kong to Beijing). Then, like children leaving home, the Kunlun's outliers scatter across China in an arc, with deep river gorges separating each child from its siblings.*

From Burma to Beijing, Asia's great rivers are born up here. The Salween seeks the Indian Ocean; the Mekong meanders through Indochina down to the Gulf of Thailand; the Yangzi yearns for Shanghai and the East China Sea; and the Yellow River yoyos its way over northern China, lifting yellow loess soil as it goes, finally giving colour and name to the Yellow Sea. Less than 300 miles separates the sources of these four rivers in the Kunlun, but their deltas are over 2,000 miles apart, and none is less than 1,500 miles long.

Fung shui *traces one of the Kunlun's offspring down to Hong Kong. By the time it gets here, it's in a playful mood, soaring and dipping over Ng Tung Shan and Tai Mo Shan, pausing briefly for breath on the springboard of Kowloon peninsula, diving under the harbour, and surfacing exultantly with a final pirouette on Victoria Peak. Sprawling across the New Territories and the outlying islands, the bones of all our other hills are joined up to this dragon child, mountain passes marking their ligaments. Along these veins of power, the force of* ch'i *flows, infusing this little corner with energy and vitality to a degree which perhaps nowhere else in China possesses.*

CHAPTER IX.

LAM TSUN, PAT HEUNG AND PING SHAN.

In this chapter we are going to leave the high hills, and betake ourselves to the fertile valleys and lowlands in the north-western part of the New Territories. They are practically the only areas of level ground in the Colony, and are the richest farm country. One of the great charms of this country is its wealth of bird life; the hilltops and coasts of Hong Kong are surprisingly empty of wild birds, but the majority of the species known to the Colony have been seen at one time or another among the woods and paddy fields and marshes which we are about to visit.

The Lam Tsun Valley. This entrancing place has been well described by Dr. Herklots,* so I will be brief. It lies under the northern slopes of Tai Mo Shan, and is reached by a path which leaves the Fanling road about a mile and a quarter beyond Tai Po, at a point where a stone bridge crosses the stream to the left of the road. The corner of the path, where you turn into the Lam Tsun valley, is to me one of the gateways to romance; the hills stand around the valley, shutting it off from the busy world outside, and the villages and fields and woods have an air of immemorial calm; here, more than anywhere else in the New Territories, you will be enfolded in the deep peace of the countryside. Bird-lovers return here again and again, for most of the commoner species of birds frequent the valley, and there is always a chance of seeing a rare one; there is no greater thrill than spotting a bird which has never before been recorded in the Colony.

Behind Hang Ha Po village, in the first wood you come to as you walk up the valley, is a colony of Egrets, and in spring you may see dozens of these lovely white birds circling around their nests in the tree-tops. Beyond the wood is an open common where cattle graze and the village boys come to play; Pipits and smart little Daurian Redstarts are flitting about among the bushes, and very likely there is a Buzzard soaring high overhead. Farther up the valley there are more woods, where in summer you are pretty sure

---

* The Hong Kong Countryside, p.14.

Commentary—Chapter 9

IF YOU haven't been into this part of the New Territories, you haven't found Hong Kong yet. This is Hong Kong from a time gone by. Most of my colleagues, even the locals, have not been here, and if asked to draw a map of Hong Kong, they would represent this area in the same way as early cartographers did—'Here be dragons!'

However, wandering around these lowlands is not quite the treat it was for Graham. They've changed a lot—not by abandonment as in the far north-east, but by more intense use for vegetable farming and, worse, for industrial overspill. Some areas have been blighted by construction depots, container storage yards, car wrecking plants, and an ever-increasing variety of other uses.

The Lam Tsuen Valley was a regular haunt for the bird-watching team to whom Dr Herklots dedicated his book, *Hong Kong Birds*, in a parody of an old English nursery rhyme: 'To Harry Hutson, Edward Aylmer, Tim Taylor, Graham Heywood, Old Uncle Tom Cobley and All'. Graham sponsored a colour plate of the Chinese Koel for the December 1934 issue of the *Hong Kong Naturalist*. The magazine carried a regular 'Ornithology' column, in which Graham was named several times with sightings in the Observatory grounds, including the Chestnut-Bellied Munia, and the first Hong Kong sighting of the Pied Harrier.

If he was still here, I'm sure Graham would be in the Big Bird Race. In this annual spree, teams of four rush around Hong Kong trying to spot as many different bird species as they can within 24 hours. Lam Tsuen is one of half a dozen likely places to hear and see some of the 288 species listed in the Race since it began in 1984.

One winter a few years ago, I went orienteering in the Lin Au valley, a delightful little enclave on the southern side of the Lam Tsuen valley. The old paddy fields were hard and bare, and we ran around with lovely views of Tai Mo Shan to the south, Tai To Yan to the north and Cloudy Hill to the east. So one autumn a year or so later, I thought it would be nice to bring my girlfriend here for a walk.

It was very different. Even on tiptoe, at five feet and two inches, my girlfriend was still shorter than the grass. So I went first, hacking the grass down with karate kicks while she tagged along behind, holding onto my rucksack to ensure she didn't lose me. Goodness knows what the views were like; neither of us looked. Finally we found the path down through the woods to Sheung Tin Liu Ha. Even worse. Typhoon winds had felled trees, and forest spiders had spun prolifically. More hacking; my girlfriend was mad.

I'm fond of Tai To Yan (Big Knife Cliff), which appears as Tai Tan Yang on old maps. It has also been translated as Razor Cliff, because 'razor' in Chinese sounds the same as 'big knife'. I wonder which ridge Graham climbed from the Lam Tsuen valley? The maps, old and new, show a number of paths which I haven't tried, but I'd be surprised if any of them provide a good route now. There is a little

to hear the Koels and Barbets calling, and you may see . . . but I am poaching on the ornithologist's private domain, and will only say that if you keep quiet you may see all sorts of delightful birds. Go alone, or with a taciturn companion, if you are bird-watching, and do not aim to get anywhere by any given time.

Towards the head of the valley the hills close in, and the stream comes tumbling down over its rocky bed between banks which in March are gay with wild roses. To the left, as you look up the valley, is the deep cleft in the north side of Tai Mo Shan leading to the big waterfalls, described in Chapter III. Facing Tai Mo Shan across the valley is a lesser mountain wall, culminating in the peak known as Tai Tan Yang. This point can be reached by a fairly strenuous scramble up a spur which rises from the Lam Tsun valley almost directly to the summit. From here you can make a circuit by climbing along the invitingly narrow and precipitous ridge to the south-west of Tai Tan Yang, and so descending over gentler grass slopes to the pass at the head of the Lam Tsun valley. I remember walking down one starlit evening after climbing Tai Tan Yang, when the country people were all indoors and I had the whole valley to myself; Venus was in the south-west sky behind me, shining so brightly that I was almost certain that I saw my shadow on the ground, cast by her light.

The Pat Heung Valley lies on the far side of the pass at the head of Lam Tsun. An attractive walk of about ten miles, involving very little climbing, is to start from Tai Po and go up the main path along the Lam Tsun valley, crossing the pass, and continuing down the Pat Heung valley to Kam Tin, where you come to the road again and can catch a bus back to Kowloon.

Some way to your left as you come down from the pass into the Pat Heung valley is a nunnery, standing in a wooded defile under the great rocky shoulder named Kwun Yam, the "Goddess of Mercy". The white buildings, with their garden and lily-pond, were once hidden away amongst the trees, and had a wonderful air of quietness and serenity. One hot summer day, as I was passing by, the nuns courteously hailed me in, and provided me with water to wash in and tea to drink.

winding road up from Hang Ha Po; it's a bit overgrown and you have to push through thick bushes at the top end.

From the Fanling end, Graham's wooded hillside (mentioned in the previous chapter) leads up to Corps Ridge, but the path where you cross to the main ridge is getting overgrown. The easiest ascent now is through the Wo Hop Shek Cemetery.

It's a lovely ridge to stroll along. Although Graham gives the impression that the summit is at Pak Tai To Yan, it's obvious when you get up there that the highest point is a mile away to the southwest. The path winds left and right of the watershed, giving views to both sides, ending with a heady scramble over the crags as you descend from the summit to the Lam Kam Road.

When Graham was writing, Kam Tin in the Pat Heung Valley really was quite remote. The Lam Kam Road, the Fan Kam Road, and Route Twisk were just village tracks. The bus back to Kowloon went through either Fanling or Tuen Mun, instead of over the top as the bone-shakers do now.

The Ling Wan Nunnery is still inhabited. I wonder if any of the nuns who gave him tea are still alive. On one day when I visited, one of the nuns, about 80 years old, was learning how to write.

Kam Tin village (Kat Hing Wai) is a tourist trap now. You will be relieved of excess funds if you go in or take photos. Nevertheless, it's a good place to go and look around if you want to see what a modern lived-in Chinese walled village is like. Other villages are not so friendly; I'm told of one that even refuses entry to the police! On the road south of Kat Hing Wai is the 'brass factory', a source of cheap serviceable souvenirs for the folks back home, but hardly genuine tradition.

The past is around us in abundance in this valley, which was one of the first areas of Hong Kong to be settled by the Chinese when they arrived a thousand years ago. Dozens of old buildings are listed in Dr Bard's guide to antiquities, *In Search of the Past*, and Sally Rodwell's *A Visitor's Guide to Historic Hong Kong*. Don't limit your exploring to what they point out; the valley is a treasure trove of history, a delight on hot summer afternoons when the hills are too hard work.

Kam Tin means Golden Fields, a name reputedly given by the San On District magistrate following generous donations to a disaster relief campaign in 1587. Good harvests are no surprise, because the *fung shui* is superb. Kwun Yam Shan and Tai Mo Shan guard the valley head. Dragon and tiger stretch out on either side of the valley, their rippling bodies visible as peaks and passes on the skyline. At the mouth of the valley, heads meet and rest in the earth. Above the two heads, the Tangs are said to have built their ancestral hall, a sacred site which few would dare to disturb, even in anger, for fear of the consequences.

So far as I know, rice is now grown in only four places in Hong Kong—by Hong Kong University on their experimental farm, by a Tai Po farmer one year out of three in

When I was refreshed they showed me round some of the buildings, of which they had good reason to be proud, for they were beautifully kept. I saw the temple, with its altar and images, and the reading room, and a belfry up in a tower, where an old nun sat with a great book open in front of her and every now and then chimed a deep-toned bell which hung from the roof above.

Many of the trees are now gone, and the belfry is only an empty shell; though some of the charm of the place has been lost, the nuns are still there, cheerful and kindly as ever.

Below the nunnery you come down to a stretch of several miles of flat and rather uninteresting country, until you reach Kam Tin at the lower end of the valley. This is a picturesque group of walled and moated villages standing amongst orchards. In the early days of the British occupation of the New Territories, the people of Kam Tin offered some resistance to the foreigners, and the fine wrought-iron gates of one of the villages were captured and taken away to England. In 1925 these gates were restored to their original position with some ceremony, and there they can still be seen along with a commemorative tablet.

Kam Tin has been inhabited from very early times; most of the villagers belong to the Tang clan, which is said to have settled here nearly a thousand years ago. Readers interested in the history of the place are referred to "Legends and Stories of the New Territories", a series of articles by Mr. Sung Hok-p'ang appearing in the "Hong Kong Naturalist".

The Lam Tsun and Pat Heung valleys are the richest rice-producing districts in the Colony. In early spring the paddy fields are ploughed and irrigated; great ingenuity is shown in the methods of irrigation, the water being led from some stream, often a considerable distance away, and distributed by a system of dykes and sluices. Sometimes you will see terraced rice fields on an arid hillside where it would seem almost impossible to obtain the all-important water.

Ling Wan Nunnery and the Tang Clan

Ling Wan Nunnery was built by three brothers of the Tang clan in about 1430, at their stepmother's request. As Mr Sung and others tell it, in the late 1300s, the Tangs allied themselves with Ho Chan, the powerful warlord of Guangdong province, supporting him with a private army, and receiving land and limited power of their own in return. It seems that Ho moved most of the Tangs out of Kam Tin into other parts of the New Territories and southern China where they could control some of his other allies who were less reliable. Kam Tin was left to the clan's junior branch, which had only two sons, Tang Hung-yee and Tang Hung-chi. Ho Chan ordered his niece to marry Hung-chi.

In 1393, the warlord fell foul of the emperor and was executed for treason, together with his whole family. The Tangs escaped punishment, but Hung-chi was ordered into exile because of his link by marriage. However, he didn't yet have any sons, so Hung-yee, who already had three sons, volunteered to go instead. After three years in exile in Manchuria, at the opposite end of China, Hung-yee set out for home. Penniless, he only got as far as Nanjing, where he died many years later after a wealthy scholar rescued him and gave him work as a clerk.

Shortly before his death, he married the scholar's daughter. They had a son, his fourth. His new widow carried his ashes and his son to Kam Tin. She was greeted suspiciously by Hung-yee's first three sons, who by then were all fully adult and married with families of their own. They finally accepted her tale, but tragedy struck: the little boy died.

Heartbroken, his mother vowed to renounce the world and serve Buddha. The hill behind the nunnery which her stepsons built was later named after Kwun Yam, the Buddhist Goddess of Mercy. Hung-chi never did have any sons, so the Tangs of Kam Tin are all descendants of Hung-yee and his first wife.

When Ho Chan died, the other branches of the clan, whom he had relocated earlier, feared that their gains under his patronage would be reversed with his death. Each branch thus began to look for ways of securing their position. The Tai Po members established the Filial Son Temple at Tai Po. The Tangs of Lung Yeuk Tau repaired an old grave which, according to the family history, housed the remains of an imperial princess who had married their ancestor 200 years before.

Perhaps the Tangs of Kam Tin saw the Ling Wan Nunnery as a way to protect themselves, and show that they were still powerful.

The rice is sown in April in a carefully prepared "nursery" of thoroughly mixed mud. Soon the young shoots come up; they are unbelievably green, and the "nursery" looks as smooth and fresh as a well kept lawn. As soon as the plants are big enough they are taken up and pricked out in neat rows in the paddy fields, where they grow in standing water. The first harvest is in June or July; the water is drained off the fields, and the rice is cut with a sickle. The sheaves are threshed by being beaten on a grating supported over a big wooden tub; it must be tremendously hard work to thresh out, sheaf by sheaf, a whole crop of rice. Then the grain is taken to the village and winnowed in a primitive wooden contraption worked by hand. Finally it is spread out in the sun on a concrete floor used impartially for drying rice, firewood or manure. The fields are at once ploughed again for the second sowing, which is harvested in October. I am always sorry when the lovely green of the growing rice has all gone from the valleys, and the fields are brown and bare until the following spring.

The Ping Shan Marshes. All along the north-western shore of the New Territories, bordering on Deep Bay and the Shum Chun estuary, is a belt of salt marshes. This low-lying land is completely unlike any other part of the Colony; although I prefer the wilder scenery of the hills, it is good sometimes to exchange the perpendicular style of landscape architecture for the horizontal, and I should imagine that those who know the fen country at home would be pleasantly reminded of it by these marshes.

There is good duck and snipe shooting, I believe, in the northerly part of the marshes, near Lok Ma Chau and Mai Pu, but this district has few attractions for the ordinary walker; the land is intersected in every direction by creeks, and though you may be able to walk dry-shod for some distance along the bunds, these meander aimlessly about and generally lead you back to your starting point before very long. So I will confine my remarks to the other end of the marsh-land, near Ping Shan, a bit of country whose chief attraction is the great variety of birds which you may see there.

crop rotation, by Green Power volunteers on an organic farm, and by an old farmer in Lantau who feeds it to his pigs; he says he doesn't know how to grow anything else, and he has rejected offers to have it marketed in Central as expensive organic rice.

Changes in land use have produced new problems. For example, the end of rice farming meant abandoning the old water catchment systems. Networks of ditches around the fields used to trap and retain summer rain, releasing it slowly over the year to ensure a constant supply. The rainwater still falls, but the ditches aren't there. So where does it go? Predictably, the rivers flood every so often, despite extensive civil engineering works to try to control them. Exacerbating the problem is the recent rapid spread of an Amazonian weed that proliferates in the summer sun and chokes the waterways.

The Ping Shan Marshes are a treasure trove. Isn't it ironic that Graham writes off the Mai Po end of the coastal area, and extols the Ping Shan end? Forty years on, it's the other way round. The birds have moved from Ping Shan to Mai Po, where the Worldwide Fund for Nature administers an internationally-renowned nature reserve. Unfortunately the reserve is jeopardised by Shenzhen across the border (water pollution from the city, and noise pollution from the new airport), Fairview Park on its back doorstep, and most recently Tin Shui Wai, the new town over at Ping Shan.

Ping Shan village is a gem—its old buildings include the restored Shut Hing Study Hall, a renovated ancestral hall in the market place, and the pagoda to the north. The pagoda, built to improve the *fung shui*, used to have seven storeys, but the top four blew off and were never replaced. I am curious about the effect on the *fung shui*; did changes in the environment render rebuilding unnecessary or possibly even damaging? Now the highrises of Tin Shui Wai are going up only a hundred metres away— good *fung shui* has 30 storeys now. You used to have to walk past some stinking ponds to reach the pagoda, but smell doesn't seem to be an important part of *fung shui*.

Ping Shan was nearly the site of Hong Kong international airport. *Hong Kong Eclipse* recounts the events of 1945:

Air services were restored at the enlarged Kai Tak airfield. It was considered to be still inadequate and the Air Officer Commanding was told to look for a new site for an airfield to serve both civil and military purposes, for which £150,000 was allocated from British Government funds. He chose the Ping Shang area in the New Territories where site formation began and a granite-quarry opened close by to give 600 tons of stone a day. However the proposed runway of 6,000 feet by 150 feet was well below the accepted international standard of 8,000 feet by 300 feet which was regarded in London as essential, and the work was therefore stopped in March 1946 and the project eventually abandoned.

Graham doesn't even mention the three hills behind this coast, but I love them. From north to south they are Hadden Hill, Snowdon (337 metres), and Kai Keung Leng. Walk

Ping Shan village is close to the road between Castle Peak and Yuen Long, about a mile and a half short of the latter. A sign board indicates the path to the village, which is out of sight of the road behind the hill on which the police station stands. It is a prosperous-looking little town, with several large houses built around shady courtyards, and a pagoda—the only old one in the Colony, as far as I know. This is an unpretentious little three-storied affair, with ladders leading up inside from one floor to the next, and narrow windows from which you can survey the country round.

Ping Shan Pagoda

The pagoda stands at the far end of the village, and beyond it are the marshes. At first sight they do not look very interesting—a wide stretch of grass and coarse rice, with water buffalos grazing here and there; (it is as well to give these creatures a wide berth, if only to avoid the look of extreme scorn which they bestow on any European). But if you keep your eyes open you may soon see what appears to be a post sticking up out of the grass in the distance, which turns out to be the head and long neck of a Heron. The wary old bird keeps his eyes on you, and before you can get near him he takes off with heavy beats of his magnificent wings, and flies away to a more secluded spot. His smaller cousins, the Egrets, also frequent the marshes; the Great Egret is a very lovely white bird, only a little smaller than the Heron himself. You will very likely see a Marsh Harrier beating to and fro over the fields in search of prey, and perhaps a Peregrine, the most accomplished flier of all the hawk tribe. On one memorable occasion I saw a small flock of Plovers

them in that order, starting from Dills Corner and descending to either Shek Kong direct from the summit, or the Castle Peak Road at the end of the western ridge. It's a day's walk, with views and guaranteed solitude. I wonder if the names of the first two were transposed: Hadden Hill is a miniature of the Welsh Snowdon, whereas Snowdon is nothing like it.

Kai Keung Leng (Rooster Ridge) is legendary. Tales go back to the Tang family's arrival in Kam Tin. Lo Hsiang-lin also calls it Heng-t'ai Shan (Level Platform Hill). Below the lower western top (374 metres), the first Mr Tang founded a school, the Li-ying College, which is mentioned in the articles by Sung Hok-p'ang which Graham refers to on page 108. Sung's articles were originally published in 1935–8 while Graham was co-editing the *Hong Kong Naturalist*, and have now been reprinted in Volumes 13 and 14 of *JHKBRAS*, 1973 and 1974. Kwai Kok Shan (Kwei Tree Horn Hill) is another name for the whole ridge. Sung says the 'horn' in the name 'referred to the two peaks of the hill that look like a pair of horns'.

According to Sung, Kwai Kok Shan is one of the 'five famous hills of San On'. The Kwei Tree in the name is osmanthus or cassia, a symbol of success in the Imperial Civil Service examinations. The slopes of the hill were said to have been covered with Kwei trees; 'the teachers are supposed to have sent their pupils out from the school to pluck the sprigs of flowers with the idea of encouraging them to further effort', he writes.

Almost at the top of the hill are two big rocks one on top of the other looking like huge grinding stones about 50 Chinese feet tall, with a passage through. A family of tigers are said to have lived there once, so it is called Lo Foo Ts'z T'ong, tiger hall. The floor of the cave is quite smooth with a lot of small stones almost like a mosaic.

Another name for the hill according to Sung was Ngo T'aam Shaan, Turtle Pool Hill, because of a hillside pool in which turtles used to live. Another story said there was a rock shaped like the head of a big turtle. This reminded students of the graduation ceremony in the Imperial exams, when the top graduate was led up the palace steps to a carved stone turtle at the top; standing with his foot on the stone, he was known as 'Sole Occupant of the Turtle's Head'. The Li-ying scholars used to amuse themselves by standing on their own rock and shouting 'I am the only man to put his foot on the head of the turtle!' Perhaps they were also bragging mischievously; 'turtle-head' is slang for the penis.

Sung says the pool was also called Virtuous Girl Pool, in honour of a very beautiful girl who was parted from her companions while out cutting grass, and attacked by a young man. Unable to attract help, she jumped into the pool to save her virtue and was drowned. The 1819 Gazetteer (*New Peace County*) had an entry for Kwai Kok Shan: 'On top is a rock called "Immortal Maiden at her Toilet"' —maybe the same girl.

Lau Fau Shan is the centre of the local oyster-eating industry. Vast piles of discarded shells litter the

in flight; their cry was exactly like that of the English Peewit, and the sound of it took me back instantly to spring days at home when the Peewits were circling and calling above their hidden nestlings.

The path follows the east bank of a broad creek until it brings you to a collection of thatched hovels standing on a high bund, built to keep back the sea. Beyond the bund, when the tide is out, there are miles of mud-flats, sometimes populated by great numbers of Herons and Egrets. You may also come across Water Hens here, and perhaps if you are lucky a Little Grebe —the Dabchick of English streams, or something very like him.

Continuing westward along the bund, you will come to some rising ground dividing the marshes from Deep Bay. Among the villages and groves here there are some rare birds; this was where we first saw the Ruby Throat, a lovely little species of Robin never before recorded in the Colony. His vivid colouring gave him away, for our attention was attracted by the patch of bright ruby-red on his throat as he moved about in a thick bush. Flower Peckers, the smallest of the Hong Kong birds, frequent one of the groves, and Pelicans, which are among the largest, have been seen in this district. I once had the good fortune to see four Great Crested Grebes swimming and diving in Deep Bay, not far from the shore; they are winter visitors to Hong Kong, and so we have no chance of watching their wonderful courtship ceremonies, which are as expressive of the joy of life as a Skylark's song.

Turning southward for a mile or so along the rising ground, you can make a circuit back across the marshes to Ping Shan, steering for the pagoda in the distance.

The Dragon Boat Festival, which takes place on the fifth day of the fifth moon, is a great occasion in this district. Every village in the neighbourhood sends a boat, and twenty or more of them assemble at high tide in a creek near Yuen Long. The crew of one of the boats seems to consist of the whole male population of the village; there are about fifty oarsmen, sitting in two rows and wielding their paddles with a tremendous show of energy but remarkably little propulsive effect. Amidships is a man with a drum and another with a

The Khud Race

The Gurkhas must think that Hong Kong is too flat for them, because they've organised a race up and down Kai Keung Leng, which they call the Nameless Hill. The race starts from the col to the north (002885) at a height of 140 metres, and goes to the summit at 585 metres, just over two kilometres there and back.

The Gurkhas are fast. The record is an astonishing 15 minutes and 12 seconds, set in 1981 and 1985 by Sergeant Gobinda Rai of the 10th Gurkha Rifles. How do they do it? Major Philip Mould, a Gurkha officer, told the Hong Kong Standard *in October 1989:*

They are under a lot of physical strain until they get to the top, then it's exactly the opposite, they have to gambol down as fast as they possibly can. They need very strong ankles, knees, and thighs to support their body weight, which is gathering momentum all the time. It's very painful. . . . From a Brit's point of view, you can keep on your toes for perhaps the first 200 yards. Then it's very much head down and a slog with your hands on your knees, pushing, pushing, pushing all the way to the top.

Two women took part for the first time in 1989, finishing in just over 30 minutes.

In the 1950s, the Khud Race was longer, but probably not quite as tough because there was less climbing. Runners started at Tam Mi Camp, ran up the valley to the col where the modern race starts, but then turned north and went up Snowdon to 337 metres before returning to the Camp, a total distance of about eight kilometers. The 1951 Khud Race, between two Gurkha teams and two British teams, was won by Lance-Corporal Jaibahadur Gurung of the 67th Gurkha Field Squadron in a time of 31 minutes and 14 seconds.

gong, beating the time, (an idea which might add considerably to the excitement of the Oxford and Cambridge boat race); the village schoolmaster is generally seated in the stern, and numerous small boys are perched wherever they can find room, hard at work baling. The boats do not race, for there is not sufficient room, but they row past each other with much flourishing of paddles and firing of crackers. On shore there are stalls, selling buns and Watson's fizzy drinks; a crew which comes ashore for refreshment will not forget to feed the dragon figure-head of their boat with a bun.

Eventually the boats form up in line and process along the creeks to the bridge below Kam Tin, where there is further excitement, for the bridge is a low one and the tails of the dragons are high out of the water, and can only be coaxed under it with much pushing and shouting. The procession ends at Kam Tin, where there are more refreshments for the thirsty crews. Altogether it is a very jolly-bank-holiday affair.

roadsides, the beach, and the fields. The oysters aren't as good as they used to be, I'm told, because pollution from Shenzhen is permeating Deep Bay and poisoning them. Shenzhen's western suburbs are visible from Tsim Bei Tsui's Lookout, worth a visit when you explore this corner of Hong Kong. A splendid flight of wooden steps led a generation of tourists up to the top to view the other side of the Bamboo Curtain. The steps, gradually decaying, won't be repaired or replaced—hardly anybody comes here now. Maybe visitors will come again when people start living in Tin Shui Wai.

A couple of miles south is Kai Shan, another little hill with a disproportionate view. From here you can see industrial estate, nature reserve, old village, new town, fishing, farming, manufacturing, and a lovely backdrop of hills all around. The sea inlet between the Lookout and Kai Shan forms the western end of the network of fish ponds and dirt tracks and mangrove swamps that is home to thousands of birds.

CHAPTER X.

WEST OF TAI MO SHAN.

Castle Peak (1,906 feet). I am afraid I can never treat Castle Peak with due respect; it looks well from the matsheds across the bay, but from farther north the ridiculous little pointed summit perched on the imposing bulk of the mountain gives it none of the dignity which its name would imply. Perhaps the weather has something to do with these reflections; each time I have made the ascent has been in late summer; damp mists hung about the mountain, and when at last I had dragged myself limply to the top I was rewarded with little or no view.

There has been a monastery on Castle Peak from very early times, although it is probable that none of the existing buildings are of any great age, and the present Buddhist community was founded only thirty years ago. The monastery stands about a third of the way up the mountain, on the side overlooking Castle Peak Bay. It is visited by many Chinese, and you will have no difficulty in obtaining a sampan to row you across the bay, and a chair to take you up the hill to it. If you prefer to walk, there is a path which leaves the Yuen Long road at San Hui, and skirts round the shore of the bay past the South China Brickworks, until it joins the other route at the foot of the hill. The paved approach leads steeply up through the woods and under an attractive modern gateway to the monastery buildings. These consist of several pavilions and temples standing among the trees on the hillside. There you may see the monks at worship, or sit in a shady arbour and drink tea while you look out over a wide view.

Behind the monastery there is a track going straight up the mountain to a little summer-house standing on the topmost ridge. From here it is only a short scramble to the summit, reached in about an hour and a half from the road. I have not seen the view from the top; it must be an extensive one, and the stately hills of Lan Tau, so like a Hebridean island, would show up well across the water. Apart from these, the country along the western borders of the Colony cannot compare in scenery with the wild beauty of the hills around Tolo Harbour and Port Shelter.

Commentary—Chapter 10

CASTLE PEAK, Hong Kong's only real holy mountain, deserves better. It was the first Hong Kong hill to be mentioned in Chinese records, and it's had at least six other names— Goat Ditch Hill, Mount Pei To, Good Omen Hill (it was declared holy by the new Emperor in AD 969 after the fall of the Tang dynasty), Holy Mountain, Green Mountain, and finally, Tuen Mun Hill.

This mountain, remarkable for the fine view it affords, has near its summit a monastery occupied by Tauist priests. The mountain is reckoned one of the eight wonders of the Canton province. Several of its large granite boulders are said by the priests to represent various mythological monsters; and several springs well up near the top, which are also esteemed supernatural wonders by the Chinese. The mountain is often visited by students and literati, and its wonders and beauties have been celebrated by them in many verses.

'A Notice of the Sanon District', read by the Rev Mr Krone, before the China Branch of the Royal Asiatic Society, 24 February 1858, and reprinted in *JHKBRAS*, Volume 7, 1967.

Chinese scholars have always visited holy mountains. An inscription 'high mountain, first in merit' was carved on a summit rock by either a famous Tang dynasty scholar or the Song dynasty scholar who established the Tang family at Kam Tin; the original is lost, but there is a replica on a stone tablet behind the monastery.

The former name Mount Pei To came from a famous Buddhist priest, Pei To, who was also known as the Tea-cup Navigator on account of his habit of carrying a tea-cup, in which he miraculously sailed across rivers. Pei To was said to be Castle Peak's first abbott.

In Graham's time, the sea came in as far as San Hui village, the only settlement. Perhaps 10,000 years ago Castle Peak was an island, separated from the rest of Hong Kong by a channel from Tuen Mun to Ping Shan.

Castle Peak is a nice scramble from behind the monastery. The hills to the north make a day's pleasant ridge walk, ending above Ling To Monastery, also part of the Pei To legend. From Yuen Tau Shan, I came down the ridge east of Ling To, past the biggest Chinese grave I've ever seen, just above the road.

The land west of Castle Peak looks intriguing, but it's an active firing range and the map warns of unexploded shells, so be careful. There is also a police training area out here, with a mock village for sharpshooting practice.

To sample the result of man wrecking his environment, try the coastal walk from Tuen Mun Ferry Pier to Nim Wan. Recipe for disaster: take an industrial estate, a council tip, a cement works, the Castle Peak power stations A and B, a partly-built highway (carefully designed to give maximum offense to the landscape), a sewage disposal scheme, the Castle Peak pulverised ash lagoon, container depots, the Nim Wan reclamation, and hilltops 'improved' with ugly concrete drains. Mix ingredients as tastelessly as possible. Dump on a remote stretch of previously unspoilt coast. Garnish with billboards, metal fencing, mud, rubbish, and assorted industrial effluent. Serves us right for not taking care.

The Tai Lam Hills. Between Castle Peak and Tai Mo Shan is a long confused range of barren hills; there are no outstanding summits, and the range offers little attraction to the mountain climber. There are, however, some delightful walks along the valleys and over the passes. The Castle Peak road runs between these hills and the sea; I wonder how many of the hundreds of motorists who go rushing by on a fine week-end know of the lovely spots they could reach within ten minutes' walking from the road. There is one expedition in this district, the walk from Orme's Bungalow to Kam Tin, which for variety of scenery is hard to beat. A little way beyond the Dairy Farm roadhouse on the Castle Peak Road is a bungalow overlooking a waterfall on the right of the highway. If you scramble up the hillside and round to the back of the bungalow, you will find a path which enters one of the most delightful valleys in the Colony. Keeping at first high up on the eastern slope of the valley, the path regains the stream about half a mile from the road; here there is a pool from whose lip the water spills over in a long cascade down into a gorge below—an admirable place for a bathe on a summer evening after work. Hidden away in the upper reaches of this stream are three lovely waterfalls, only to be reached by a rough scramble over the rocks.

At Easter time there is a fine show of rhododendrons along the banks of the stream, and Bamboo Orchids grow in the damp places among the rocks. Higher up I used occasionally to see a pair of Eagle Owls, magnificent great birds with a wing-span of five feet.

The path leaves the stream at the pool and continues up a subsidiary valley to the pass at its head, where an old pine tree once marked the way over into the next valley. This is the valley which reaches the coast at the Brewery. Its upper part is deep and narrow; the path, now only a rough track, runs along the hillside high above the stream, crosses a pass over the ridge to the north, and comes out on a wide cup among the hills, where the headwaters of yet another stream wind through abandoned paddy fields. The track disappears, but if you follow the stream upwards for twenty minutes or so you will come to a well-marked path crossing the valley at right angles to its length.

The Tai Lam Hills were unknown territory to me for a long time, but now I have visited them several times, on each visit gaining a greater appreciation for their subdued charms. Don't judge this area by the Maclehose Trail sections, for they unaccountably are the worst it has to offer. Tai Lam Chung Reservoir divides it into two blocks, both trending WSW-ENE.

The north-west block culminates in a 507-metre top, unnamed on the map but called Chiu-ching Shan (Nine Path Hill) by Lo. From the pavilion half way up the Tuen Mun Trail (076798), a path goes east along the northern slope of the block, down into the valleys and up over the ridges, till you reach the hill overlooking Wong Nai Tun Reservoir. It isn't marked on the 1990 Countryside Series map, which is odd because it's an obvious track. Delightfully quiet, wooded valleys reward you on this walk; nobody ever lived or farmed in these hills. They remind me of Wales or the Appalachians.

The south-eastern block is more complex. An excellent way to reconnoitre it is to visit the two Fire Lookouts, at 978799 (look in the hut for an old photo of the view) and 000805. From these two points, you can see the whole area and plan your walks.

Graham's expedition is tricky now. Orme's Bungalow is on the promontory between Ting Kau Beach and Lido Beach. Graham's valley ends in Lido Beach, but it's so changed that I just can't see 'one of the most delightful valleys in the Colony'. The catchwater siphoned off water from the lower part of the stream; below, squatters settled; above, jungle flourished; then came the Tuen Mun Highway. A road goes up from Ting Kau to the catchwater, about forty metres above Graham's old swimming pool. Then it goes west and emerges where he did, by some graves high above the Sham Tseng stream. The track up to the head of the valley (984787) is there on the old map, but trees have been planted all over it. If you can get up another way, you'll find the 'wide cup among the hills'. This valley, with Sheung Tong above it, is one of my favourites; I've spent lazy hours sprawled by the brook, watching the sky overhead and listening to the silence. The right angle path junction (990795) leads up to a pass (988798), but according to my old map Telegraph Pass is a mile away at 005802. I think Graham got it wrong.

Alternatives for the first part of this walk start from Tsing Lung Tau (try and fit in a visit to Yuen Tun, where the old village has been made into a museum) or Sham Tseng. Or you could walk from Tsuen Wan, over Shek Lung Kung (Stone Dragon Arch), which has a marvellous tawny colour in winter, contrasting beautifully with the blue sky. On your way, you pass the source of the Lido Beach stream.

Turning to the left up this path, a short climb brings you to Telegraph Pass, the third and highest pass on the walk, reached in an hour and a half from the Castle Peak road. As you top the rise the scene changes; behind are the bare hilltops and shrubby valleys of the mountain country; in front the ground falls away to the fertile plain of the Pat Heung valley, merging in the distance into the level salt marshes around Deep Bay.

The rest of the way is plain to see, and a walk of an hour and a quarter will bring you down from the hills and across the paddy fields to Kam Tin. From here you can get back to Kowloon by bus, changing at Yuen Long.

At the eastern end of the Tai Lam range, under the shadow of Tai Mo Shan, is the waterwheel valley, which has already been described in Chapter III. If you continue upwards past the waterwheels, keeping always to the west of the stream, you will reach a secluded upper valley where there is a Buddhist settlement. Two of the charming and courteous people of this place once showed me round their home, which consisted of a cave under a huge overhanging boulder. A thatched porch shaded the wayfarer as he sat and drank tea (and how very refreshing Chinese tea can be when you are out walking). Inside was the living room with beds and a table and a little shrine, all kept spotlessly clean, and down below was an underground kitchen, supplied with a clear trickle of water through a chink in the rocks.

And now we have completed our circuit of the New Territories, and returned to our starting point at Tai Mo Shan. I have said something in these pages of the wild life of the country—the birds and fishes and flowers. But no mention has been made of the mammals, the reason being that they are nearly all nocturnal and the ordinary walker hardly ever sees them.

Tigers sometimes visit the Colony in winter, coming down from the mountainous districts in Chinese territory, though not so often as the "tiger stories" in the newspaper would lead one to suppose. Leopards are also occasional visitors; one was killed near the Bride's Pool a few years ago. The commonest resident mammal

Pre-war Deforestation

Villagers always kept the hillsides fairly barren. Annual fires and grass cutting were traditional activities, and did not cause great concern so long as they did not upset the balance by becoming too extensive. In the 1930s, commercial pressures did start to upset the balance, and a series of angry letters to the editor of the Hong Kong Telegraph, *such as this one on 11 January 1938, raised the topic of vandalism:*

Sir,—I feel sure that residents who appreciate the beauty of Hongkong must view with profound concern the work of organised gangs who are denuding the hillsides of trees. Thousands of pine trees have been cut down in the New Territories, and there are vast areas, where but a few years ago trees were flourishing, which now present a pitiful vista of stumps. If this ravaging is to be stopped, and surely it can be, severe penalties must be imposed upon those who are engaged in the trade. Furthermore, the number of forestry guards must be increased, and daily raids made. I suggest that no person should be permitted to carry firewood without a written permit, and that firewood merchants who encourage the despoilers by purchasing their wood should be dealt with severely as receivers of stolen property.

Unless drastic steps are taken at once, the damage done to the Colony's hillsides will take many years to repair, and the health of the community will suffer in consequence. To come across a tree-cutter at work a few years ago was unusual, and a warning shout was enough to send him scurrying away. Today, these people are to be seen working in small gangs, and if spoken to, show a brazen disregard to any protest made. The problem must be tackled immediately and sternly. To fine a few of the culprits is not enough. A sound thrashing when caught in the act would prove a better deterrent.

OLD RESIDENT

These activities were a precursor to even more damage during the war, when almost all Hong Kong's trees were cut. The authorities wanted timber for construction, and local people were desperate for fuel, even though they were forbidden to go out on the hills.

The luxurious vegetation cover that we see today is post-war growth. Possibly the last area of native woodland left undisturbed by either man or fire is above Tung Chung in Lantau, on the slopes of Lantau Peak and Sunset Peak. Now even this is threatened by the new airport, a proposed reservoir, and a new town for 200,000.

is the Deer, which is said to be abundant in the New
Territories and on Hong Kong Island, though it is rarely
seen in daytime. You will often come across deer-
traps on the hill paths; they usually consist of a sapling
bent over the path and held down by a cord with a
noose in the end of it. The noose is concealed in a
grass-covered pit in the path, and arranged so that
when the deer puts its foot into the hole it releases a
catch, allowing the sapling to spring back and draw
the noose tight around the deer's leg.

Wild Pigs frequent the dense thickets on some of
the shrub-covered hillsides, such as the north face of
Ma On Shan, and are feared by the villagers for the
damage they do. Parties sometimes go out pig shooting
with a mixed pack of village dogs.

Civets and Wild Cats also occur, and Wolves,
Foxes and Otters are probably still here, though they
are becoming rare. And lastly there are two queer
beasts, the Pangolin, or scaly ant-eater, and the
Porcupine. The latter sometimes appears in front of
the headlights of a car at night, usually to the great
astonishment of the driver. I have always wanted to
see these two creatures, but have never succeeded in
doing so, for they are very shy and only come out after
dark.

Apart from one or two species of mice, which lead
a precarious existence owing to the abundance of snakes,
this exhausts the list of the Colony's mammals.

CHINESE BLUE MAGPIE

Post-war Afforestation and Water Supply

Bill Smyly recalls that when he arrived in 1954, the hills were barren of trees and he could walk pretty much anywhere he wanted. Other long-time residents have said the same. Old soldiers on nostalgia visits are surprised at the amount of greenery, both in the valleys and on the hills. In their days, the mountains were brown, and amongst the paddy fields there were neither trees nor hedges. They also remember the smell of the human excreta that was used to fertilise the fields, and sometimes made exercises memorable.

Widespread tree-planting began after the war and still continues, designed more to control erosion than to supply timber. Many hillsides now display a pretty mix of species. The modern tree cover is quite different from the old.

Walkers will encounter catchwaters all over Hong Kong. Most of the modern planting has taken place above the catchwaters, on land where no other planting or cutting is allowed. The catchwaters were built at various times to cope with one of Hong Kong's oldest and most constant problems—how to ensure a reliable water supply.

In November 1960, the Shenzhen authorities agreed to sell water to Hong Kong, and started to construct the Shenzhen Reservoir and the pipeline across the border. But before they were finished, Hong Kong was forced to import its first water.

'A severe drought in 1963 reduced water-supply to four and even three hours supply every four days, and tankers were chartered and brought million gallons from the Pearl River', according to the Hong Kong History Pictorial (Tai Dao Publishing Ltd., 1990). Times were desperate in 1963: residents of 45–7 Second Street, Western, were afraid to use water when their house caught fire; and visiting ships brought drinking water from Japan, the Philippines and Taiwan.

June's newspapers carried daily reports of progress, as a 6,000-foot-long pipeline was laid from the Caltex Terminal Pier on Texaco Road, Tsuen Wan to Shing Mun. Workers moved to Sham Tseng to lay another pipe from the San Miguel Brewery Pier to Tai Lam Chung Reservoir. On Monday, 24 June 1963 the chartered Liberian tanker 'Ianthe' left Hong Kong to collect 3.7 million gallons from higher up the Pearl River, returning late on Wednesday night to start piping the water up to the reservoirs.

CHAPTER XI.

HONG KONG ISLAND.

Living in Kowloon with all the New Territories at my back door, I am afraid I do not know the Island as well as I should. It is a lovely place—perhaps one of the loveliest in the world; every newcomer to Hong Kong must have marvelled at the beauty of the harbour and city at night, and when the time comes for me to leave here for good I shall take with me some treasured memories of this wonderful island.

I shall dream of cool bathes at Shek O on summer evenings after the heat of the day, when the sunset colours were in the sky, the encircling hills were darkening from green to indigo, and the brown sails of the junks out to sea were catching the last rays of the sun. One or two belated surf-bathers might still be sporting about in the big rollers, which had travelled, for all I know, right across the Pacific on the trade winds. And as we turned for home the lighthouse on Waglan would begin to wink across the water in the gathering darkness.

Or of sailing into Aberdeen harbour when the fishing fleet was coming home, steering the dinghy tack by tack up the narrow channel along with the great junks, and watching them haul down their sails and slip into their appointed anchorages with perfect precision.

Or of evenings spent at some friend's house, when we would sit after supper on the terrace, high above the moonlit sea, and watch the sampan lights twinkling far away in the distance under the shadowy outline of the Lemas.

Yes, it is an enchanting place, and yet when I am out walking on the Island I can seldom capture the romance of wild country. It is all too tamed and respectable; the paths are mostly so well kept and so neatly edged with concrete, and too often I come across villas and water-works and golf courses. So I shall not have a great deal to say about the walks on the Island, as it is easy to find your way without a guide-book.

The Peak and High West. With the aid of the Peak tram, the top of Victoria Peak (1,770 feet) may be reached with but little exertion on your part.

Commentary—Chapter 11

No OTHER island in the world has such an instantly recognisable name: Hong Kong! Isn't it magic? On my first visit here, I was seduced into staying by two things—a walk on Sunday from The Peak to Braemar Hill, and lunch on Monday at the Yacht Club. On both occasions, the harbour was a temptress. There isn't a day goes by when I don't gaze out of my twenty-fifth floor harbour-front window in awe and amazement at the wonder of it all. What a magnificent testimony to both God and Mammon.

I'm surprised to see that Graham doesn't mention my favourite hill. I'm going to leave it that way, for in the middle of the energy and bustle all around, I prize the peace and quiet that I find up there. It's the only hill around this fantastic harbour that survives without modern attachments; there isn't a road up to it; and the view is outstanding. Long may it remain undisturbed, and me with it.

Victoria Peak has three tops, all captured since Graham's time by telecommunications pirates. According to Lo Hsiang-lin, it was originally named Tough Top Hill. In 1810 it was renamed Tai Ping Shan (Pacific Peak, or Peaceful Peak) to commemorate the peaceful final surrender of pirates led by the seven sons of Cheng Lien-ch'ang, the devil of Devil's Peak. All seven had adopted their father's profession, and the frustrated Manchu authorities and foreign traders finally had to collaborate to defeat them. Lo takes a chapter for their story, ending with some of the landmarks, such as the Man Mo Temple, which are associated with them. The modern Chinese name for the hill is Che Kei Shan, Torn Flag Hill, or much more commonly Shan Teng, The Peak.

Beside the path up the west ridge of The Peak there is a rock on your right, labelled 'The Governor's Stone'. I've no idea why it's called that, or what its history is. Nobody else I've talked to has ever known of its existence.

High West is nearly always climbed now from the junction of Lugard Road and Harlech Road. It's not clear from either the old map or the new map whether the west ridge route could be followed all the way without zigzagging.

For the most part, you can walk on Hong Kong island just as Graham described. The valleys and hillsides around the reservoirs at Pokfulam, Aberdeen, and Tai Tam have been designated country parks, as has most of the Shek O peninsula. Hopefully, this means they won't be redeveloped, and we'll be able to continue enjoying them.

I'm reluctant to make recommendations, because that attracts people to come and walk, which brings noise and litter, both of which I loathe in the countryside. So even though Graham and I both identify some of the most delectable spots in Hong Kong, I'm not going to tell you which they are. You'll find them when you search, and they'll be all the more rewarding for the quest.

On a sunny Sunday afternoon, you might visit Mount Davis, which had a heavy gun emplacement

The superb view from the summit gains enormously from its contrasts, for on the one side you look down on to the roofs of the city far below, and the busy harbour with its anchored ships looking like toy vessels on a miniature pond, and on the other the eye ranges over a serene expanse of sunlit sea to the distant line of islands on the horizon to the south. Lugard Road, which encircles the upper part of the Peak, commands these grand views, and provides a pleasant walk of about two miles along the level, starting and ending at the upper tram station. A scramble of a few minutes from this path will bring you to the top of High West, a fine mountain with steep cliffs falling away on each side of the summit ridge. A more energetic way up High West is the exhilarating climb up the far ridge of the mountain, which rises above Mount Davis Gap on the Island Road.

A walk which has the merit of being entirely down hill is to start from the upper tram station and take the narrow road which winds down through the woods to the south to Pokfulam Reservoir, joining the Island Road at the Dairy Farm. About half way down there is a forestry path branching off to the right; this will take you along hillsides where the bell-flower blooms at Chinese New Year, across the flank of High West, and so to a point above Mount Davis Gap, whence it is an easy descent to the road.

Around Wong Nei Chong Gap. The starting point of several excellent walks is Wong Nei Chong Gap, on the bus route between Hong Kong and Repulse Bay. The charming ride known as Black's Link begins here, at first running westward along the slopes of Mount Nicholson and then crossing the watershed and rounding the northern side of Mount Cameron to Wanchai Gap, where it rejoins the road. This is a walk of about an hour, during which you are very likely to see the Blue Magpie, a handsome fellow with a scarlet beak and a very long tail, familiar to every Peak dweller. He is a noisy bird, with a harsh scolding cry which only faintly resembles the cheerful untuneful laugh of his black and white cousin. From Wanchai Gap a road runs down southward past the reservoirs to Aberdeen, or you may return to your starting point by a rough track over the summits of Mount Cameron and Mount Nicholson, a switchback ridge-walk to set the blood running on a cold day.

Belcher and His 'Prosaic Names'

Many of Hong Kong Island's Western names were bestowed by Captain Sir Edward Belcher, R.N., captain of HMS Sulphur, when he conducted the first English survey in January and early February 1841. His book Narrative of a Voyage Round The World, *published in 1843, mentions the survey only twice, both times briefly:*

On the return of the commodore on the 24th (January 1841), we were directed to proceed to Hongkong, and commence its survey. We landed on Monday, the 26th, at fifteen minutes past eight, and being the bona fide first possessors, her Majesty's health was drank with three cheers on Possession Mount . . . . .

Having completed the necessary data for the survey of Hong Kong, we quitted for Macao, intending to rate the chronometers, and complete a course of magnetic observations, preparatory to revisiting Manila, on our homeward route.

He named dozens of features after himself, but only Belcher Bay and Hill Above Belcher's survive. His colleagues did better.
• Mount Kellett: Lieutenant H. Kellett was the captain of Sulphur's sister ship, HMS Starling.
• Mount Gough: Major-General Sir Hugh Gough commanded the British troops during the siege of Canton in March 1841.
• Mount Johnston: A. R. Johnston, the first deputy governor, became notorious for holding the first land auction without permission.
• Mount Nicholson: Nicholson was the midshipman of HMS Sulphur.
• Mount Parker: Rear-Admiral Sir William Parker, K.C.B. was Commander-in-Chief Far East from August 1841.
• Mount Collinson: Sir Richard Collinson was a lieutenant on HMS Sulphur.
• Pottinger Peak: Sir Henry Pottinger, Bart., was the first governor.
• D'Aguilar Peak: Major-General G. C. D'Aguilar became commander in the early 1840s.
From the ships, we get Sulphur Channel, Starling Inlet and Hebe Haven. Lamma Island's highest hill was also named after one of the British captains, Sir H. Le Fleming Senhouse, of HMS Blenheim, but his hill at some stage acquired a 't' and became Mount Stenhouse.
Other hills named in a similar way include Mount Davis (Sir John Davis was the second governor), Mount Cameron (Major-General W. G. Cameron commanded the army in the 1880s), Mount Butler, and Bennet's Hill. Butler and Bennet have resisted my researches.

One of the pleasantest short strolls on the Island is to take the path eastward from Wong Nei Chong Gap, which goes over the hills and down to the Ty Tam reservoirs, joining the Island Road at the big dam. Another path which starts from the same point is Sir Cecil's Ride; this is so determined to have no ups and downs that it takes an enormously long and twisting course along the 700 foot contour above Tai Hang and Quarry Bay, eventually bringing you to the pass between Mount Butler and Mount Parker. From here it is only a short descent to Ty Tam reservoir, whence you can make your way down to the Island Road, or return up the hill to Wong Nei Chong Gap. Instead of descending from the pass, it is possible to continue south-eastward to Ty Tam Gap by a very delightful little track which winds in and out of the woods on the southern slopes of Mount Parker.

It is unfortunate that nearly all the hills on the Island have been given such very prosaic names. Ben Nevis, Scafell Pike—even the names can fire the imagination; Ng Tung Shan has a sonorous ring about it, befitting a fine mountain; but Mount Butler and Pottinger Peak convey not a spark of romance, however worthy their namesakes may have been. Where a native name exists it is surely better to stick to it. In the Himalayas, Everest is I believe the only mountain called after an Englishman; it is lucky that the name sounds so well, though the native one Chomolungma, "The Goddess Mother of the Snows", is perhaps more beautiful and certainly more appropriate.

The Southern Slopes. This side of the Island does not seem to have suffered much from the ravages of woodcutters, and most of the lower hillsides are still well covered with trees or scrub. Many attractive places are within easy reach of the Island Road, which follows the coast more or less closely around the south side of the Island.

Aberdeen, of course, is always worth a visit, to stroll through the village and see the harbour crowded with fishing boats of all sizes.

A mile to the east of Aberdeen a branch road leads to Little Hong Kong and Shouson Hill. A short distance above this road is a catchwater flowing along the lower slopes of Mount Nicholson and Mount Cameron. Many

Aberdeen

Photo. Kaan Chee Leuk

beautiful flowering trees and shrubs grow in the thick woods bordering the catchwater.

I have never climbed Violet Hill, which rises steeply behind Repulse Bay Hotel, but Stanley Mound, overlooking Repulse Bay on the east, can easily be climbed up its south ridge from the Island Road, and is a good viewpoint.

Shek O. The road out to Shek O takes a high place among the many lovely motor drives in the Colony. I like to dawdle along this road in August, when the graceful blue harebells are in flower all over the hillside above Ty Tam Bay. For the walker, Pottinger Gap path provides an attractive short cut from Ty Tam Gap to Shek O; the path starts at a signpost a hundred yards or so east of the junction of the Shek O and Island roads, whence a walk of about a mile, mainly downhill, will bring you to Big Wave Bay. A friend and I were once amusing ourselves by bowling rocks over the cliffs near here, when we disturbed a nest of hornets. They left me alone and concentrated all their fury on him, with the result that he was badly stung and very nearly rushed violently down a steep place into the sea. This tale has a moral—if you must bowl rocks down cliffs, do so in company with one of those unfortunate people who always get stung by insects.

Another good walk in the neighbourhood is along the narrow road which runs from Windy Gap (well named, for once) out to the end of Cape d'Aguilar. There you can sit, preferably out of sight of the wireless station, on this miniature Land's End, and watch the big swell come rolling through Beaufort Channel and break in white foam on the rocks below you. It is as well to return by the same way, for, though it is possible to get back to Shek O along the eastern side of the peninsula, it is a very rough scramble indeed through the thick scrub which crowns the cliffs of this wild bit of coast.

Before closing this chapter I would like to have said something about the flowering trees and shrubs which grow in greater profusion on the southern slopes of the Island than anywhere else in the Colony. Few of them, however, possess English names; I do not know their Latin ones, and must refer you to the books on the natural history of the Colony mentioned in the introduction.

during the war; the ruins of the fortifications are still there to be explored. There was another gun on Hill Above Belcher's, but that's nowhere near as intriguing.

Around Wong Nai Chung Gap, Mount Cameron was the site of a War Memorial which the Japanese started to build during the war; It was finally demolished at 4.30 p.m. on February 26, 1947, reported by the *South China Morning Post* as 'TO-DAY'S BIG BANG . . . . . 'Eye-Sore' To Be Razed With Explosive'. From the photos I've seen, it was a job well done. Hardly anybody climbs the hill now, so it's very overgrown. Climbers are attracted to its neighbour, Mount Nicholson, by crags on the south ridge.

Sir Cecil Clementi, the governor from 1925 to 1930, was married to Lady Clementi. From the Gap, where Sir Cecil's Walk goes north, Lady Clementi's Ride goes south and traverses the slopes of Nicholson and Cameron. Both routes are popular with joggers and walkers, and provide gentle family strolls with almost no vertical effort.

Bowen Road is another flat and popular route. It's flat because it used to be an aqueduct carrying water piped through the hill from the first Tai Tam Reservoir (the upper one) to a tank above Central. You can still see original stonework at the sides of the road. From Stubbs Road, above the entrance to the Aberdeen Tunnel, there's a fine view of the arches below Lover's Rock where people come for their morning *tai chi* session. Good *fung shui*.

Sir Cecil's Ride twists around the slopes of Braemar Hill and the northern extension of Siu Ma Shan (Pony Hill). According to Lo Hsiang-lin, this used to be called Hung Hsiang-lu Shan (Crimson Censer Hill), on account of a red incense burner (or censer) which came 'floating on the sea from some distant place' and used to be displayed in the Tin Hau temple below in Causeway Bay.

On the southern slopes, Tai Tam Country Park contains some beguiling but inaccessible hills. Violet Hill and Stanley Mound are both accessible (the latter gets more eroded every year), but The Twins who separate them are unfriendly, and will scratch. The catchwater round their western flanks, between Wong Nai Chung Gap and Stanley, is very scenic. One word of advice—don't end up in Stanley late on a summer Sunday afternoon; the queues and the traffic crawl back to town make a frustrating end to the day.

The road out to Shek O is the route for the No. 9 bus, which is usually driven by the winner of the 'Hong Kong's Craziest Bus Driver' contest. Try it—remarkably, the buses don't often crash, and it's an unforgettable experience.

From Tai Tam Gap, the map tempts you with a 'major footpath' up Mount Collinson—but I haven't found it yet. Obelisk Hill, too, is tempting but overgrown. Dragon's Back is fine. D'Aguilar Peak has been captured by several different bands of telecommunications pirates.

CHAPTER XII.

LAN TAU ISLAND.

The distant silhouette of Lan Tau Island closes the view westward from Hong Kong Harbour; the twin summits of Lan Tau Peak itself are hidden by nearer hills, and one would little imagine that the island contains by far the finest mountain scenery in the Colony. Lan Tau always reminds me of Skye; on both islands the hills rise straight from a rocky coast to a height of over 3,000 feet, and the little villages sparsely scattered along the shore are dwarfed by the great bare hillsides behind them. The fishing harbour of Tai O might almost be Portree, and Lan Tau Peak might be Sgurr nan Gillean. But once one sets foot on the hills the resemblance vanishes; here is no heather, no springy turf, no keen air from over the moors, and none of the soft colouring of a Hebridean landscape. Lan Tau has its advantages, though; the sun is brighter, the weather finer, and the flowers and shrubs more luxuriant than in its chilly northern counterpart. Here you can walk in a singlet and shorts, or bathe and picnic in warm sunshine, which you can seldom do in Skye.

Like Skye, most of Lan Tau Island is difficult of access and little visited; I can never set out for either of these delectable places without a mild sense of adventure. The ideal way to visit Lan Tau is with a private launch, and for the yachtsman the island has many possibilities. A night spent at anchor in some little bay under the towering hills is a memorable experience. I have also tried camping on the island, but the armies of ants which marched over us all night spoilt an otherwise delightful trip.

Ferry steamers run between Hong Kong (vehicular pier) and Silver Mine Bay, at the eastern end of Lan Tau Island, calling on the way at Ping Chau Island, a busy little place where there are lime kilns and a match factory. This ferry service will give you some five hours on Lan Tau—long enough to explore the old silver mine a little way up the valley, or to climb the imposing hills overlooking the bay, but too little time to ascend Lan Tau Peak itself, which is situated some five miles to the west of Silver Mine Bay, over difficult country.

Commentary—Chapter 12

I ALWAYS think of Lantau as Hong Kong's 'even though' island. Lantau is still a treat, even though it's considerably tamer than in Graham's day. The hills are still wild, even though somebody has invented a 'Lantau Trail'. The journey is still an adventure, even though the ferries from Central are frequent. There are still remote and sparse villages, even though China Light & Power were only just dissuaded from building a new power station on the south-west tip of the island. The islanders, for the most part, were in favour; it was outsiders who stopped it.

The future doesn't look green. Hong Kong's new airport will be built on the north coast, with a new town for 200,000 people. Discovery Bay has spread further every time I go.

Skye is a better bet for the lover of adventure. Sgurr nan Gillean has kept its privacy better than Lantau Peak, for all there is a plan to let people go over the sea to Skye on a road bridge. Incidentally, there was a plan a few years ago to buy an island off the west coast of Scotland, to which Hong Kong people could escape from China's clutches after 1997; what a rum idea.

Lantau's a fine place still when you get away from the crowds and use your imagination. Like anywhere else in the world, that mostly means avoiding the Sunday hordes and the barbecue sites. For the adventurous walker, there's plenty of scope. The hills are still there (though a few might have to be demolished to comply with international airport standards), dotted with secluded temples and monasteries, where life has probably changed very little even in this century. I'm still looking for the place referred to by Sarah Rossbach in *Feng Shui*: (E.P. Dutton. Inc., 1983): 'A cliff on Lan Tao . . . resembles a naked man with an erection and is said to prompt exceptional flirtatiousness in the girls of a nearby village.'

You wouldn't think it now, but Lantau used to be the most populous and important island on this stretch of coast. Tai O was a metropolis; Tung Chung and Fan Lau were important military posts. The Brits had a look at Lantau in 1840 before deciding which island to steal. I suppose the residents of Lantau would have kicked up the same sort of fuss that the farmers of Wong Chuk Hang and Chek Chue did at the time.

Would Lantau have thrived the same as Hong Kong? Imagine Tai O as Central, Tung Chung as Causeway Bay, Shek Pik as Aberdeen, and Cheung Sha Wan as Stanley. Hei Ling Chau has been flattened, turned into a housing estate, and connected with a bridge to the Chi Ma Wan/Silver Mine Bay Industrial Reclamation. More reclamation has brought Castle Peak as close as Tsim Sha Tsui. Hard to imagine, isn't it? Have you seen the plans for the new airport? Look at them, and you'll see that this is a mild sort of vision. So visit Lantau soon.

Our maps name both Sunset Peak and Rocky Top. Rocky Top is Lin Fa Shan (Lotus Flower Hill). Sunset Peak has an alternative name Tai Tung

135

Another ferry leaves Hong Kong very early in the morning, calls at Castle Peak, and goes on to Tai O and Tung Chung on Lan Tau. This enables you to spend a long day on the island, and to climb Lan Tau Peak from the west or north, returning by the same ferry in the evening. If you wish to explore the island thoroughly, you can spend a few nights either at Lan Tau Camp or at the monastery on the plateau, but arrangements have to be made beforehand.

Sunset Peak and Rocky Top. These two peaks are nameless on the map; Rocky Top is the square-topped mountain overlooking Silver Mine Bay, and Sunset Peak lies between it and Lan Tau Peak. Both can be climbed without difficulty from Silver Mine Bay. From the beach where the ferry passengers are landed, a good path leads through a village and across a short stretch of level ground to the foot of the hills. There is no mistaking the route, for it is the way to the camp, and a well-made path, clearly visible from below, climbs the south-eastern shoulder of Rocky Top. It is a long steady grind up to the ridge, here about 2,000 feet high. Turning right-handed at this pass, a further 500 feet of climbing up the broad grassy ridge will bring you to the summit of Rocky Top. It is a good viewpoint; away to the east across the water lies Hong Kong, with its hills rising clear above the smoke haze which covers the harbour; to the west the eye ranges across a deep wooded valley to an amphitheatre of splendid hills. The accompanying sketch was made from near here.

The path to the camp continues westward from the pass, climbing at a comparatively easy gradient around the shoulder of the ridge on which stand the huts. The latter are superbly situated at a height of about 2,500 feet. Beyond them a track continues up the ridge to the summit of Sunset Peak (2,858 feet), the third highest point in the Colony. Opposite, across a deep gap in the ridge, stands the impressive pyramid of the Lan Tau Peak, now quite close and filling the whole view to the westward.

Returning by the way you came, you will be in time to catch the afternoon ferry back from Silver Mine Bay to Hong Kong.

Photo. H. Hubert

The Start of the Climb. Lan Tau Island

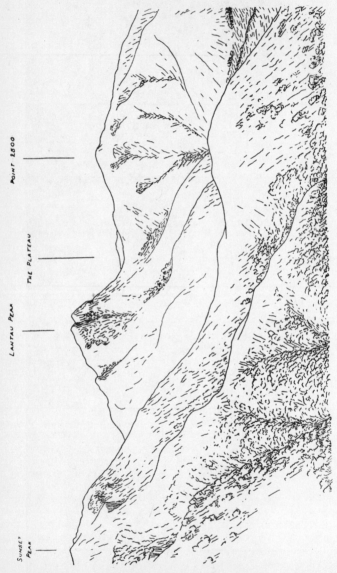

SUNSET PEAK — LANTAU PEAK — THE PLATEAU — POINT 2800

Lan Tau Peak from the North-East

Shan (Great East Peak), and the modern mapmakers have added Yi Tung Shan (Second East Peak) in between.

Few people now bother to walk across the fields, preferring to catch the bus up to Nam Shan and save themselves the first 100 metres of climb. So I, perverse as ever, usually go across the fields. The way isn't signposted through the villages and I get lost. But I still do it; the old path is such a nice start to a walk, getting away from the people and the road so quickly.

The old path joins the Lantau Trail just above the road at Nam Shan, and from there on Graham's notes are fine. This is how the *Hong Kong Sunday Herald* of 16 July 1939 reported improved access to the camp on the ridge east of Sunset Peak:

The Public Pavilion at Silver Mine Bay built by the Hong Kong and Yaumati Ferry Company, Limited, was formally opened yesterday in the presence of 300 visitors, including prominent Chinese and European personalities of the Colony, by the District Officer north, Mr. A. J. Cruttwell . . .

The improved ferry service and the opening of the Pavilion should greatly encourage the Public to visit the summer settlement near Lantau Peak. It is situated at nearly 3,000 feet above sea level and the climate is excellent. It has an ice-cold fresh-water swimming pool. Mountain chairs and bearers are available.

Somewhere in the stream to the north of the camp is Perfect Pool, a secret bathing place where Graham used to take his daughters.

Lantau Peak from Tung Chung is still possible, but rarely done since there are easier ways of doing it.

Taking the Tung Chung bus to Pak Kung Au saves about 330 metres, reducing Lantau Peak to 600 metres and Sunset Peak to 540 metres. Steps further reduce the effort required. The Trail is easy to follow, and you have to try very hard these days to get lost or fall off the overhanging crags.

When you're experienced, check out the south-western ridges of Lantau Peak, called Kau Nga Ling (Dog Tooth Ridge). Where Graham left the summit and turned off after scrambling down for 300 feet, there's now a path that continues straight ahead. A prominent notice warns you not to proceed any further. A similar notice confronts you if you start at the bottom end, from the contour path above Shek Pik Reservoir. It's good advice—this is a hands-out-of-pockets scramble, with some exposure above long steep slopes sweeping down into the gullies far below. I have been up this ridge twice, but not down. When it's this steep, I much prefer to go up.

This is the way I went one Boxing Day. At the top we almost had icicles on the ends of our noses; it was one of the most wintry days I've had here. If you're nervous or inexperienced, don't try this route.

Graham's notes for the route from Tai O seem superfluous now that his path has been replaced by a road. I love Tai O's setting. The hills to the east—Cheung Shan (Elephant Hill), and Sz Shan (Lion Hill)—form such an impressive backdrop to the town. From the road, the south-western end of Sz Shan presents an enticing array of rocky outcrops; it looks as though you could go up . . .

Lan Tau Peak from Tung Chung. The only easy
ascent of Lan Tau Peak is up the long east ridge of the
mountain, which rises from the low pass between the
latter and Sunset Peak; it is the ridge appearing to the
left of the summit in the sketch. Our party had fore-
gathered in the small hours of the morning, and
motored out to Castle Peak to catch the ferry there,
wondering sleepily what on earth had possessed us to
get up at such a fantastic hour. We ate our breakfast
on the upper deck of the ferry, and relapsed again into
uneasy slumber on the hard and draughty benches as
the first grey light of dawn was beginning to show in
the sky. Life began to be tolerable when we reached
Tai O, for by then it was full daylight. The sky was
dull and overcast, and I thought regretfully of a
previous arrival here on a morning of exquisite beauty,
when the sun was rising over the mountain tops and
beginning to stir the mists which hung over the little
harbour, while the junks lay mirrored in the still water,
each one sending up a curl of blue smoke to announce
that breakfast was preparing.

Before proceeding to Tung Chung the ferry usually
waits for half an hour or so at Tai O, while sampans
some alongside to disembark passengers or to load the
cargo of big tubs containing fish of all shapes and sizes,
alive and dead. It was a rather sleepy party which
landed at Tung Chung at half past eight. First we
went to look for the old fort in Tung Chung village,
which lies about half a mile to the south of the landing-
place, across the paddy fields. We found the fort
among the houses at the foot of a wooded knoll overlooking the village; an archway brought us into a
square space, now occupied by cottages and trees,
surrounded by a great stone wall, many feet thick.
Several clumsy old muzzle-loading guns still point sea-
wards through the creepers which cover the top of the
wall. A friend has translated for me a copy of the
Chinese inscription on one of the guns; it runs as
follows:—"Made in the first moon of the tenth year
of the Emperor Chia Ching; weight 1,200 catties." The
weight presumably refers to the gun and not to the
Emperor. This gives the date of the casting of the gun
as 1806. It is said that the fort was originally a pirate
stronghold, and was occupied for a time by the British
when the island was taken over.

. . here . . . . . then here . . . . . and round there . . . . . I nearly missed the bus doing this.

There is some lovely country south of Tai O. I persuaded a colleague at the office to bring her boyfriend and join me one misty February weekend. Crossing Tai O Road at Milestone 11, the Lantau Trail heads for Ling Wui Shan. On the ridge we found extra strength in the wind, so I visited the top of Kwun Yam Shan alone. There are little statuettes of Kwun Yam on the trig point, and a couple of bells; I rang one a few times for luck. We plodded along the ridge through the mist, stopping for two or three breakfasts on the way. Chocolate brownies were produced; the day felt better. We left the Trail at Fan Shui Au to look for Tai Hom Sham, which for me was the whole point of the walk. Orienteering skills, dead reckoning, and faint traces of forgotten paths got us to the summit. As we stood in the mist congratulating ourselves, the clouds blew away to reveal our little corner of Lantau and the Pearl River delta. Heaven smiled. Thank you, Kwun Yam.

Forswearing the direct descent, we retreated to the pass and the security of the Lantau Trail. The mist closed in again as we left the top. Down the hill towards Tai O, we stopped to explore the gardens at Lung Tsai Ng Yuen. We croaked to the invisible frogs and put our noses in the roses. Curiously, although the air was sweet with their scent, none of the individual blossoms had any fragrance.

It's a good day's walk round the southwest coast from Shek Pik to Tai O. You may take longer than you expected, especially if you allow yourself to be distracted by the rock carving, the Obelisk, the Fan Lau fort and stone circle, the beaches, and the sights of Tai O. It's probably better to do it this way round, though, because you can't always get on the bus if you're not in the queue at Tai O.

On the north coast, I've done bits between Tai O and Ngau Kwu Long. Each time I go, progress has marched over a bit more. Ngau Kwu Long has now been 'improved' with a new concrete path over the hill from Silver Mine Bay; it announces itself as the North Lantau Pedestrian Dual Carriageway, or something grandiose like that. Most walkers turn left towards Tung Chung, past the old 'sohool' above Pak Mong, which must have been a marvellously quiet place to study. If you turn right and go down to Tai Ho Wan, you'll find a minute little beach, and a secluded temple where devotees still live and worship.

Next to the beach beyond the temple, a track goes up the back of Lo Fu Tau (Tiger Top). Discovery Bay residents have made new tracks on their side, which confuse walkers trying to find the way with the old map. A flight of steps opposite Seabee Lane, signposted to the Lookout, goes over the knoll overlooking Disco Bay and down the other end, which is where the path to the summit starts. I think it would be quicker to start from that end in the first place. Apparently, people get even more confused doing the walk between Discovery Bay and Silver Mine Bay. Paths have proliferated like rabbits, and

Leaving Tung Chung, we made our way across the paddy fields towards the foot of Lan Tau Peak. The path crosses the main stream by a concrete bridge, then leads up a valley to the low pass at the foot of the east ridge of the mountain. Near the head of the stream below the pass we halted for a nondescript meal which might have been a second breakfast or a first lunch. The remaining 2,000 feet of ascent to the summit are up a track which keeps close to the skyline of the ridge; on the one hand steep scrub-covered slopes fall to the roofs of the monastery above Tung Chung; on the other you look down precipitous gullies to the wild southern coast of the island. Some large boulders perched insecurely on the edge of the abyss proved too tempting for us, and were duly dislodged and sent crashing down the hillside—a most reprehensible amusement.

We reached the summit (3,065 feet) soon after 1 p.m.; the ascent had taken 3½ hourse exclusive of halts. Although it was a grey day and the clouds were close above our heads, the view was a magnificent one. Instead of returning to Tung Chung, we decided to cross the mountain and go down to Tai O, as the ferry calls here later and we should thereby gain an additional two hours on the island. From the summit one looks down on a plateau on which stand the buildings of a Buddhist settlement, and the path from the plateau down to Tai O is in clear view. The most direct way off the mountain would seem to lead over the lower of the twin summits and so down a spur to the plateau. This is a bad route; a band of overhanging cliffs, invisible from above, crosses the spur 500 feet below the summit; though one can avoid these rocks by bearing away to the left, the whole slope is extremely steep and is covered with boulders, every one of which seems to be ready to start at the slightest touch on a headlong career towards the valley.

Instead we scrambled down for 300 feet or so along the crest of another spur which descends at an easy angle in a south-westerly direction from the higher summit. On our right was the gully below the gap between the two peaks, and we soon found a rough track leading down into this hollow. We halted in a sheltered place by the side of the little stream; the descent had been steep and exhausting; we drank of the stream, settled ourselves comfortably among the

Chung Yeung

The ninth day of the ninth lunar month has been an important one for the Chinese for many centuries. On it they observe the custom of 'climbing high', and the Peak Tram does its best trade of the year. The reason for the upward surge is contained in an old legend told by Hugh Baker in Ancestral Images Again *(South China Morning Post Ltd., 1981):*

It tells of a soothsayer who warned a virtuous scholar of a terrible calamity impending. 'Hasten!' said he to his friend, 'with all your kith and kin, climb to the shelter of the mountains, till there is nothing between you and the sky, and take with you food and drink.' The scholar thanked his counsellor and followed his advice, carrying with him a paper bag containing food, and a jug of chrysanthemum-wine. Returning at the end of the day, he found his cattle and poultry had died a violent death. 'That,' said he to his family 'would probably have been our fate, but for the warning.'

Fung Shui and Mountains

What is fung shui? That's a tricky question, and I'm not an expert. To become an expert you have to apprentice yourself to an existing master and get years of experience. But fung shui is too important to ignore. Dr Joseph Needham, an authority on the history of Chinese science, explains that: 'Every place had its special topographical features which modified the local influence of the various ch'i (energies) of Nature. The forms of hills and the directions of watercourses, being the outcome of the moulding influences of winds and waters, were the most important.'

There we have the relationship between landscape (mountains and rivers) and fung shui (winds and waters). In The Living Earth Manual of Feng Shui *(Routledge & Kegan Paul Ltd., 1982), Stephen Skinner writes that fung shui is 'the art of living in harmony with the land, and deriving the greatest benefit, peace and prosperity from being in the right place at the right time'. The fung shui practitioner's attitude to mountains reflects their dominant position within the pattern of nature. With his advice, one can maximise favourable influences and minimise the unfavourable ones.*

Mountains exert their influence through position and shape. The relationship of one hill to another is a display of the complex balance of yang dragon energy and yin tiger energy. The landscape is a playground. In Skinner's words, 'mountains are the traditional abode of the immortals, of dragons, and of gods.' Mountains' shapes represent the five elements (fire, wood, earth, metal, and water) and the five planets (Mars, Jupiter, Saturn, Venus, and Mercury). Other influences include birth dates and stars.

The best site for a village, house, or tomb is thus determined primarily by how best to draw on the dragon and tiger energies where and when they flow freely, whilst avoiding conflict in shape. Ernest J. Eitel, the first

Continued on page 145

143

rocks, and went to sleep. Time slipped by, and it was not until 4 p.m. that we continued the descent.

Beyond the gully the path becomes easier, skirting across the hillside to the plateau. The Buddhist settlement here is situated nearly 2,000 feet above sea level, and must be a bleak place in winter. A broad path, winding down through delightful scenery, took us from the plateau to Tai O, a distance of four miles. We reached the harbour at 6 p.m., and were being rowed out in a sampan to the ferry, when to our dismay it hove up its anchor and put to sea without us. After such a good day the prospect of a night on the island and a very late arrival at our office desks next day was not attractive; the police sergeant at Tai O came to our rescue, and by his kindness we were enabled to get across to the mainland and so home that night.

From Tai O. The mountain may be crossed in the opposite direction to that described above, starting from Tai O and coming down to Tung Chung; the foregoing notes should enable you to follow the route without much difficulty. The only real problem is to find your way out of Tai O; only a few of the houses stand on dry land, and the rest of the town of 7,000 inhabitants consists of a maze of wooden shacks and superannuated sampans built on stilts over the mud-flats, and intersected by waterways. I always lose my way in this picturesque place; it is best not to attempt to pass through it on foot. Instead, take a sampan from the ferry steamer and row up the main street of the town (for in Tai O most of the streets are waterways). If you are like Mr. Rat in "The Wind in the Willows", and love "just messing about in boats", Tai O is the place for you. There are boats everywhere—anchored in the harbour, scurrying up and down the creeks, being built on the slipways, or spending a restful old age shored up on the mud and converted into dwelling houses. And all the people are connected in some way or other with boats; they are building boats, or sail-making, or repairing fishing nets. The sampan takes you through the village and up a creek beyond; if you land at the head of the creek, you will find a path leading towards the only opening in the hills which encircle the harbour.

COMMENTARY

European authority on fung shui, *analysed Hong Kong's prospects in his classic book,* Feng Shui, *first published in 1873:*

The peak of Hongkong, presenting the outlines of Jupiter, is under the influence of wood. Now at the foot of the peak there is the hill called Taip'ingshan, with the outlines of Mars, and therefore the representative of fire. Now, a pile of wood with fire at the bottom—what is the consequence? Why, it is no wonder that most fires in Hongkong occur in the Taip'ingshan district.

A Reading List

Here are some books I consider worthwhile:

• *Magic Walks*, Volumes 1, 2 and 3, by Kaarlo Schepel (The Alternative Press, 1990, 1990, and 1991). Good basic guides to lots of easy walks.

• *Twelve Hong Kong Walks*, by Derek Kemp (Oxford University Press, 1985). One walk for each month; lots of informative botanical notes, but can be confusing.

• *Time Out Collection*, by Barry Girling (TV and Entertainment Times, 1990). Exploring villages, temples, other odd spots, and one or two hills. Clear directions. Attractive.

• *Another Hong Kong*, edited by Alan Moores (Emphasis (HK) Ltd., 1989). More encouragement to explore odd spots, but again, few hills.

• *Journal of the Hong Kong Branch of the Royal Asiatic Society*, or JHKBRAS (Royal Asiatic Society, annually since 1961). A treasure trove for local studies and history.

• *In Search of the Past*, by Dr Solomon Bard (Urban Council, 1988). Fruits of a lifetime spent exploring history. Bit awkward to handle, but do take it with you.

• *A Visitor's Guide to Historic Hong Kong*, by Sally Rodwell (Odyssey, 1991). Easy style, readable and informative. Another to take out with you.

• *Hong Kong and its External Communications before 1842*, by Lo Hsiang-lin (Institute of Chinese Culture, 1963). Study of pre-British Hong Kong.

• *Hong Kong Legends*, by Chu Wai Tak (Kam Ning Publishing Co., 1988, in Chinese).

The path at first follows the bottom of a deep valley, keeping to the left of the stream; then, as you climb out on to the higher ground, the summit of the mountain comes gradually into view, guarded by slopes. which look forbiddingly steep. The monastery on the plateau is reached in about two hours from Tai O; rising immediately in front of you, and obviously unclimbable, is the impressive north-west spur of the peak. The summit can however be reached by following a rough track, which, as already mentioned, slants away across the hillside and into the gully to the right. A steep scramble up the far slope of the gully brings you on to the crest of the south-west ridge, and so by easy walking to the summit. Time 3½ hours from Tai O.

The descent down the east ridge and along the valley to Tung Chung can be made in time to catch the ferry, which, by the way, does not anchor at the head of the bay where the stream flows into the sea, but in the channel between Lan Tau and Chu Lou Kok island.

A shorter expedition, which takes you through splendid scenery but misses the top of Lan Tau Peak, is the walk from Tai O direct to Tung Chung, crossing the pass on which stands the Buddhist settlement to the north-west of the peak.

Round the Horseshoe. No walk in the Colony can excel the scramble over the magnificent semicircle of peaks which stand around Tung Chung. Starting at the eastern end of the horseshoe, following the skyline right round to Lan Tau Peak, and descending to Tai O, the whole walk is rather over 12 miles in length and includes about 5,500 feet of ascent. A long and glorious day; the times given below are moderately fast ones, for there is little time for dawdling if you are to catch the ferry at the end of the walk.

Landing at Tung Chung at 8.30 a.m., I took an obvious path up the steep spur which overlooks the eastern side of the bay. Dog roses were in bloom. around the foot of the mountain, and the sunny slopes above were gay with flowering rhododendrons. A climb of 1,500 feet or so brought me on to the ridge, and the remainder of the walk was over high ground with wide and lovely views on either side. The ridge

nobody's sure which way to go.

From Disco Bay, you can also walk over Tai Che Tung northeast towards Ma Wan. I got muddled on the start of this walk until I was on the tops. The map shows a path up to Yi Pak Au from the road north of Disco Bay, to the right of a stream. This is not the first path you find as you walk along the road. On your left are six highrise blocks, two sets of three. Don't take the path you can see between these two sets, even though it goes up to the right of the stream; it reaches the ridge about 300 metres above and to the left of the pass. Keep going through the big gate onto the construction site for the next set of highrises (you may have to duck under the gate). Over to your left is an embankment. On top of it, in the middle, is the path to Yi Pak Au. From the pass, you can go as far as you want on a sequence of energetic ups and downs. I think there would be a continuous path back along the northern shore to Siu Ho.

Chi Ma Wan peninsula is the last bit of Lantau's coastline. Here is a startling juxtaposition of experiences. Start at the Chi Ma Wan Detention Centre, where Vietnamese boat people are kept like caged animals in a zoo. Finish at the Frog and Toad in Tai Long Wan, where jolly crowds let off steam at weekends, and the annual Mud Wrestling Olympics brings together afficionados of the bizarre for a celebration of decadence.

Round the Horseshoe: The first time I tried this splendid circuit was in mid-summer. Failing to find Graham's 'obvious path up the steep spur', which my friend Ruth

and I thought would be at 028672, we took the path north of it from 028674, round the back of a hut where we surprised a naked man enjoying the sun.

As we bashed our way up the hillside through the summer vegetation, the sun shone, and we perspired freely. After two-and-a half hours, we had drunk all our water, and had got about 300 metres above the road and 300 metres from the road. We looked at each other and admitted defeat. After wetting our parched throats in the village (less than 15 minutes to get down), we contented ourselves with what turned out to be a very pleasant walk along the catchwater from Pak Kung Au to Nam Shan. Half way along we found a pool, where we lounged, and soothed our toes and spirits.

My second attempt came six or seven months later, alone, in winter, in the rain. I was surprised when the Tung Chung bus from the 7.00 ferry didn't turn off at Cheung Sha. Oh well, I reasoned, it must be the Tai O bus; never mind, I'll do the walk in reverse and finish at Tung Chung. The bus turned into Shek Pik Prison and stopped. The sign on the front said that it was now going back to Silver Mine Bay. I wandered along the beach disconsolately for a few minutes in the drizzle, until I decided that by climbing the south-west ridge, I could still do the circuit based on Tung Chung, taking the second half first and the first half second.

By lunchtime on Nei Lak Shan, (Maitreya Hill; Maitreya is the Buddha-to-come) just below the clouds, I started to realise that I'd only manage the second half, to

at first runs eastward to a broad saddle, which can also be reached by a path up from the little bay lying in a north-easterly direction at the foot of the hills. The track here turns right-handed up easy slopes to the summit of Rocky Top, where I halted for an hour to enjoy the view.

Beyond this point I followed the ridge down to the dip and up past the camp to the top of Sunset Peak. From the cairn on the summit it was necessary to bear left-handed in order to avoid a false ridge which ends in a steep spur overlooking the Tung Chung valley; the main ridge runs down in a more southerly direction from the summit. Here for the first time the path failed me, but the steep descent of 2,000 feet to the next pass was not unduly rough and could be taken at a gallop. I had now reached the low pass at the head of the valley leading up from Tung Chung, and for the rest of the way I followed the route described above.

After the morning's walk over two high summits, the long climb up the east ridge of Lan Tau Peak was a little wearisome. The top was finally attained at 2.40 p.m.; the sky had clouded over and a searching east wind was whistling through the gap between the twin summits, so after a short halt I scuttled down the western face of the mountain to the plateau. The four miles of easy going along the path to Tai O were a pleasant relief to muscles stretched and wearied by the long day on the ridge. There was no need to hurry down that charming valley; I strolled into Tai O soon after 5 p.m., and this time I did not miss the ferry.

A Walking Tour. The Colony is restricted in area, and there may seem little scope for a walking tour within its frontiers, particularly as there are no inns where one may conveniently spend the night. But a line drawn from Sha Tau Kok in the north-east to the far south-west point of Lan Tau measures over 30 miles, and a friend and I decided to make a tour along this line one Chinese New Year holiday.

Starting from Sha Tau Kok, we walked across country over the hills on the north-west side of the Pat Sin range until we reached the foot of the Lam Tsun valley. We went up this valley, and crossed the pass at

COMMENTARY

Pearl Fishing in Hong Kong

The south coast of China used to be renowned for pearl fishing. One of the best areas was Tolo Harbour. Translated by Lo Hsiang-lin, a report to a Yuan dynasty official in the thirteenth to fourteenth century described the coastal regions:

. . . the pearl-pools are situated in remote and culturally backward areas, which are usually more poverty-stricken than other regions . . . the ruggedness of the landscape and the savageness of the inhabitants in the pearl-fishing areas render it unwise for the local government to push its authority too far. The pearl fishing territory is composed of ominous mountain ranges and treacherous islands.

The report identified Lantau as one of the 'treacherous islands', and went on to clarify the character of the inhabitants: "These folks look more like beasts than men, go naked, have tongues resembling those of birds, and are capable of diving like otters."

It concluded that pearl fishing was a difficult occupation:

. . . the pearl-pool is separated from inhabited areas by more than two hundred *li* of unhealthy terrain where venomous snakes and hideous creatures live and breed, polluting the atmosphere with infectious diseases and pestilence. Communication is difficult; a double trip to and back from the civilised world takes more than ten days. With the shortage of supplies, the fatigue of marching, and the pestilential atmosphere of the place of work, it is indeed common for the men to succumb to the hardships.

A Walking Tour

Is there any walker who doesn't sit sometimes with a map, dreaming of what might be here? What would the view from there be? Could I get down that hillside? How to devise a day's walk without treading old ground?

I'm still working on my perfect Hong Kong walk. I think I've got a route which will link up all the main tops. For a long time I tried to include just the 500-metre tops, but no matter how I did it, they wouldn't connect up tidily. Then when a friend wrote a book about his journey round the 3,000-foot tops of the British Isles, it inspired me to look again, and I discovered that the 450's would just do: 52 tops, 10 days, 150 miles, and 50,000 feet of climbing.

Start on Sharp Peak. Hop across to Ma On Shan, and southwest to Kowloon Peak. Watch the city as I go west along the ridge. Swing around Sha Tin to Needle and Grassy Hills. Swing again to Tai Mo Shan, and head north over Tai To Yan. Climb Pat Sin Leng and Robin's Nest before heading south again to Kai Keung Leng, the Tai Lam Chung Hills, and Castle Peak. The ferry takes me over to Tai O and a couple of days on Lantau, ending up at Discovery Bay, and the hoverferry to Central. The final day is on the island, and the last hill is Mount Parker. From there it's back to Happy Valley, and home.

its head to the Pat Heung Nunnery. Monasteries and nunneries in China often take the place of wayside inns; travellers can lodge for the night and obtain meals, and are expected to pay only what they can afford. So we knocked on the door of the nunnery, and asked if we could stay for the night. The courteous nuns received us, gave us a good supper, and showed us into the guest room, where we made ourselves comfortable on "min tois" or padded quilts laid on the bed boards.

Next morning we were up early, for we had to reach Castle Peak by 10 a.m., in order to catch the ferry to Lan Tau. Our way led across the level paddy fields of the Pat Heung valley, and along the Tai Lam valley, which cuts a straight rift through the hills south-westward from Pat Heung, reaching the coast at Brothers Bay. It was easy going, and we caught the ferry with time to spare.

Landing at Tung Chung, we took the path up towards the monastery on the plateau, where we had arranged to spend the second night. We were heavily laden, for we expected vegetarian food at the monastery and had brought extra supplies; our rucksacks bulged with knobby tins of bully beef, the path was steep, and the sun, hitherto hidden behind the pall of grey cloud which is typical of Chinese New Year, came out in full strength. But we had all the afternoon before us, and could allow ourselves frequent halts by the wayside to cool off.

The guest-house at the monastery consists of a single very large room. The central part contains chairs and a table, while the two wings are partitioned off into sleeping cubicles. The sanitary arrangements out at the back are simple but clean. We were well looked after by the friendly monk who ran the guest-house; he served us with excellent vegetarian meals, and saw that we had plenty of quilts at night. A large and cheerful party of young Englishmen were spending their holiday at the monastery, and the guest-house that evening was filled with unwonted noise.

We set out on the following morning to complete our walk from one end of the Colony to the other. Descending by a path to the south coast of the island, we followed the shore along sandy beaches and over

Chinese Graves

Hong Kong's hills are dotted with evidence of all three burial stages that a man goes through after his death. It is vital to care for ancestors, since according to traditional Chinese belief there is an inter-relationship between living and dead which enables them to influence each other. So, as Eitel says in Feng-shui:

If a tomb is so placed, that the animal spirit of the deceased, supposed to dwell there, is comfortable and free of disturbing elements, . . . the ancestors' spirits will feel well disposed towards their descendants, will be enabled to constantly surround them, and willing to shower upon them all the blessings within reach of the spirit world.

If, on the other hand, the ancestors are not happy with their lot, it is in their power to create bad luck for their descendants. Since the landscape is a living organism, with good and bad influences, it is vital to have good fung shui advice when choosing a burial site. In the New Territories, traditional practices are still observed.

In the first stage the body, in its coffin, is buried in the family's own cemetery, often just a small plot on the hillside near the village. The temporary grave is covered with a mound of earth and cement; offerings and flowers are placed on top. In the second stage, after about ten years, the bones are exhumed, cleaned by a bone specialist, and arranged in a funeral urn, a 'golden pagoda'. Collections of these urns can be seen everywhere in specially-built shelters. Finally, in the third stage, a fung shui expert selects a place to build a permanent horseshoe-shaped tomb, in which the urn is cemented behind a name panel.

Few reach the third stage. The difficulty of finding a good site, and the expense of reburial mean that most descendants leave the urns to keep each other company. Sometimes, unexplained bad luck prompts them to build a proper tomb. Whatever stage they reach, the dead are attended by the living every spring at Ching Ming, the grave-sweeping festival. Some will also be visited in autumn at Chung Yeung.

I never know how much respect I ought to show to graves. My Chinese colleagues in the office are horrified when I show photos of graves, but my local orienteering club often uses graves as markers, and hundreds of people go bounding all over them without any concern.

Tung Chung. After lunch, as I checked out and rejected the descents to the north one by one, it dawned on me that I mightn't even manage that. Finally, at 3.30, in dense bush around the 140-metre contour on the hillside above Sha Lo Wan, I turned back to Ngong Ping and the bus.

A year later, I climbed Por Kai Shan (Mother-in-law's Hairdo Hill) from Pak Mong. That's a grand climb, especially the last 100 metres. As I came onto Pok To Yan, the rocks were painted with signs saying 'LTM'—Lantau Marathon? A clear path led away down the western ridge, to just above the point Ruth

rocky headlands, until after some hours of walking through completely wild and uninhabited country we reached the south-westerly extremity of the island. Here, on a promontory surrounded on three sides by the sea, is a mound of weed-grown stones, all that remains of a fort said to have been built by the early Dutch navigators.

On our return we rounded the end of the island, and took a path along the north-west coast to Tai O, whence we walked up to the monastery by the usual way. We spent several more nights there, amusing ourselves by exploring Lan Tau Peak and its supporting ridges, and on the last day of our holiday we walked over to Silver Mine Bay where we caught the afternoon ferry back to Hong Kong. Our little trip had been a complete break from our normal lives, for though we had never been more than 20 miles from the city, we had been right out in the wilds, and had covered new country every day.

We have come to the end of our walks together. This little book is, I feel, an imperfect guide; even if you carry it in your pocket and consult it on knotty points of route-finding, you will often lose your way. Still less can it succeed in conveying to the reader any real impression of the glories of the countryside; but then no words can do that. It will have fulfilled its purpose if it persuades a few more ramblers to set out and explore the hills for themselves. And may I urge that we who enjoy the beauties of this Colony should do all in our power to preserve them unspoilt? Hong Kong has an incomparable setting, but hitherto man has done lamentably little to contribute to the natural beauties of the place. The city sprawls untidily, with few green spaces or noble buildings to grace it, and there is a pressing danger that much of the surrounding country may be spoilt by unsightly building developments along the new roads. It need not be so; a city can be beautiful in itself, and the country can be saved from the efforts of speculative builders. Let us make sure that our successors will have no cause to revile us for leaving to them ugliness where we found so much that was lovely.

and I had struggled to a year and a half before. There is a faint track down that end, but the main track turns southwest, and emerges in Shan Ha village at 031666.

So now I could do the circuit, I think. It's a tricky start. Walk to Shan Ha from the road. Follow the path past the front of the village and round the corner of the last house. Go between the hens on your right and a water pipe on your left, through to two old banyan trees in a little square. In front of you is a big clump of bushes; to your right is a fence around a house. The path goes between the bushes and the fence. After a few hundred yards through the trees, it turns left and goes uphill. From there, everything should be clear all the way to Tai O. Sometime I'll be back to check out the lower ends of the paths up Nei Lak Shan from Tung Chung to make it a complete circuit.

What a wonderful time I've had with Graham's guide to the hills and the countryside of Hong Kong. Graham was so right, of course, in his warnings. Hong Kong has been a bad offender for pollution. The laws are feeble and unenforced. The countryside is being steadily ruined.

The sea is already a hazard to health on some of the beaches, and many people will not swim in Hong Kong waters at all.

Yet it's never too late to take some action. Our environment is bad now, and it will get worse unless we do something about it. There is already a ground swell of concern building up. I hope you add your energy to the movement. An old Chinese proverb says that 'a journey of 10,000 *li* starts with one step.'

As I wrote, I repeatedly came across saying from Kenya that gives both warning and hope: 'We think we own the world and can pass it on to our children in any state we please. Not so. We have just borrowed it from our children, and we will have to account for it when they take it back.'

Treading in Graham's footsteps, I've been horrified at times at what we've done to our children's home and property. I hope this book helps us to appreciate our privileges and duties a little more clearly. I hope it inspires us to enjoy and treasure what we have. In other words, I hope to see you rambling in Hong Kong.

Let's leave the last word to a poet, Feng Shixing:

> Good friendship after a hundred years is new.
> And now for a pleasant ramble of ten days together!
> Green precipices climb up, side by side;
> Clear cascades compete in splashing contests.
> Clouds come—ten thousand ravines are levelled;
> Winds blow—a thousand hills are shaken;
> Mysteriously a peak separates itself from the rest.
> I return home; I have fulfilled my whole life's dream.

'Temple of the Crouching Tiger', translated by Phelps & Wilmott in *Pilgrimage in Poetry to Mount Omei*.

It is said that one of the greatest of the Chinese
Emperors caused a miniature mountain to be built for
him in an empty room in the Imperial Palace. When
affairs of state prevented him from spending his leisure
among the Western Hills he used to sit for a while
on his own little mountain for rest and meditation. He
knew the right place, and there we too can find refreshment for body and spirit. A rucksack and a pair of
nailed shoes are a passport to the mountains, where our
life is fuller and our friendships warmer, and we realize
that after all the world is a good place, very fair to
look on.

Map of Hong Kong